Praise for *Disruptive Marketing*

"*Disruptive Marketing* is an incisive look at today's complete overhaul of traditional marketing and its effects on both producers and consumers. Colon has expertly analyzed the importance of breaking away from yesterday's linear and stuffy approaches and opened up new possibilities in the digital market. It's an essential read for anyone looking to make a splash with the next big thing."
—Francesco Baschieri, CEO and founder of Spreaker

"At last there's a brilliant book I can send to clients who refuse to believe that to stay relevant they need to shatter pre-conceived ideas, open their eyes, and dare themselves a little. Hold onto your hats, marketers, because this book's going to take you on the ride of your life. Through entertaining storytelling and irrefutable evidence, Geoffrey Colon has distilled what every one of us needs to know about how to succeed in this digital world. With our world's only constant being change, this book should be on every marketer's desk if they want to understand what it takes to be nimble and survive."
—Mel Carson, coauthor of *Pioneers of Digital* and author of *Introduction to Personal Branding: 10 Steps Toward a New Professional You*

"Grounded in fact, amplified by inspiration, and supported by compelling stories drawn from real experiences, *Disruptive Marketing* is worthwhile reading from beginning to end."
—Jamie Gutfreund, global chief marketing officer, Wunderman

"The pace of marketing and product innovation is moving faster than ever before. Why do some companies thrive while others wither on the vine? It's their approach to marketing and product development. In this book, Colon gives you the tools to change your thinking and approach to growth to get ahead of the curve."
—Sean Ellis and Morgan Brown, GrowthHackers.com

"Seasoned marketers are now facing more challenges than ever, as their decades of experience can sometimes be disadvantageous. This book illustrates an era where creative professionals are eschewing traditional corporate hierarchies, marketing responsibilities are being distributed widely across organizations, and consumers are exposed to brands through each other instead of through established publishers. Geoffrey Colon offers some telling examples of how pioneers are navigating this, along with a telling roadmap for many more of the changes coming in the years ahead."

—David Berkowitz, chief marketing officer of MRY

"*Disruptive Marketing* will make you realize that your marketing comfort zone will quickly become uncomfortable unless you are prepared to embrace the rapid changes that Colon so eloquently documents. This excellent book is probably best summed up by the title of its final chapter: Learn, Unlearn, Relearn."

—Diane Young, co-founder of TheDrum.com

"In *Disruptive Marketing*, Geoffrey Colon makes a case for reducing the complexity, bureaucracy, and single-minded leadership that create barriers to finding and swiftly implementing creative solutions to the challenges facing modern marketers. In the current landscape, missing the forest through the trees is no longer an option. An inability to see or unwillingness to embrace the need for change signals the beginning of the end for a marketer. Colon lays out the truth, the whole truth, and nothing but: our industry is being disrupted, and anyone who refuses to adapt will be left behind."

—Melanie Deziel, @mdeziel,
award-winning branded content strategist

"An intelligent and fun read that gets at the heart of the major problems we currently face in marketing, and how to fix them. This book belongs on your desk, and your boss's desk."

—Mathew Sweezey,
principal of marketing insights at Salesforce

"Colon offers a bold and much needed perspective to challenge the status quo that ideas can only come from traditional processes and creative-led teams. Today's ideas come from early collaboration with diverse thinkers ready to take a journey that may start off uncomfortably but ends in the most magical way. As Colon points out, the people at the table may be far from 'the expected'—and that's a good thing. (And his idea about writing the press release for the product before you create it is brilliant.) "

—Lindsey Slaby, founder, Sunday Dinner Agency

"*Disruptive Marketing* isn't so much a business book as a marketing manifesto. Its core message is that marketing isn't a set of core principles or effective practices or even a department in your organization—it's a way of thinking. And disruptive marketing borrows genius and inspiration from every industry and walk of life, imbuing everything you do and even how your existing and target customers interact with your brand. Geoffrey Colon's goal is to free us from our assumptions and one-size-fits-all thinking. He shows us that we need to focus on, and capture, what really matters: time, attention, and conversation. *Disruptive Marketing* manages to be wide-ranging, creative, ambitious, visionary, shrewd, and practical all at once—just the same qualities that, according to Colon, our marketing strategies should have."

—Holly Epstein Ojalvo, founder and editor of the digital news site *Kicker* (gokicker.com)

"Colon's exceptional career in marketing has provided him with a unique perspective and the ability to think futuristically when it comes to marketing and innovation. His book is a must read for those looking to stay ahead of the curve and the competition, especially young people launching their careers. Balancing concepts with concrete resources and tools, the book will leave you excited and prepared to launch and execute new creative marketing ideas."

—Emily Miethner, CEO and founder, FindSpark.com

"Colon successfully lays out the three intangible skills—empathy, design, and emotional intelligence—that are pivotal to disruptive marketing and thinking. These key qualities will help millennial marketers build the foundations to their careers and empower industry veterans to rethink their approaches to delighting customers. Marketers of all ages will tremendously benefit from taking a deep dive into *Disruptive Marketing*."

—Tai Tran, *Forbes* 30 Under 30, 2016 and LinkedIn Top Voice, 2015

"Colon eloquently explains through his own experience how 'producerism' is not a buzzword anymore. The art of customer co-creation is very much real! Today's audiences are not satisfied with just consuming content in a stand-alone mode. Many want to be a part of the product's journey and, in a lot of cases, be an active voice in shaping it. With increasing activity over social media, there is more to come and Geoffrey correctly surmises the most innovative companies of the future will have producerism in their DNA!"

—Rohan Khara, co-founder and COO of Jabbercast

"Colon's chapter on podcasting intertwined with his theory that anyone can be a creator/producer is key to understanding how marketing is changing. Writing not merely about brand messaging but content creations produced by many, Colon uses personal and professional experiences to drive home to the reader that marketers aren't doing your marketing; rather, everyone who loves your product is doing your marketing."

—Parviz Parvizi, co-founder of Clammr

DISRUPTIVE
MARKETING

WHAT GROWTH HACKERS, DATA PUNKS, AND OTHER HYBRID THINKERS CAN TEACH US ABOUT NAVIGATING THE NEW NORMAL

GEOFFREY COLON

Foreword by Gemma Craven

AMACOM

AMERICAN MANAGEMENT ASSOCIATION

New York • Atlanta • Brussels • Chicago • Mexico City • San Francisco • Shanghai
Tokyo • Toronto • Washington, D.C.

This publication is designed to provide accurate and authoritative information in regard to the subject matter covered. It is sold with the understanding that the publisher is not engaged in rendering legal, accounting, or other professional service. If legal advice or other expert assistance is required, the services of a competent professional person should be sought.

Library of Congress Cataloging-in-Publication Data
Names: Colon, Geoffrey, author.
Title: Disruptive marketing : what growth hackers, data punks, and other hybrid thinkers can teach us about navigating the new normal / Geoffrey Colon ; foreword by Gemma Craven.
Description: New York : American Management Association, 2016. | Includes bibliographical references and index.
Identifiers: LCCN 2016005635 (print) | LCCN 2016015447 (ebook) | ISBN 9780814437391 (hardcover : alk. paper) | ISBN 9780814437407 (eBook)
Subjects: LCSH: Branding (Marketing)
Classification: LCC HF5415.1255 .C65 2016 (print) | LCC HF5415.1255 (ebook) | DDC 658.8/27–dc23
LC record available at https://lccn.loc.gov/2016005635

About AMA

American Management Association (www.amanet.org) is a world leader in talent development, advancing the skills of individuals to drive business success. Our mission is to support the goals of individuals and organizations through a complete range of products and services, including classroom and virtual seminars, webcasts, webinars, podcasts, conferences, corporate and government solutions, business books, and research. AMA's approach to improving performance combines experiential learning—learning through doing—with opportunities for ongoing professional growth at every step of one's career journey.

For Allison, Olive, and Matilda. xoxo

"The most disruptive thing in the market is not technology, but rather the customer."

—TIFFANI BOVA

"Species go extinct because there are historical constraints built into a given body or a given design."

—KEVIN KELLY

"Get into the habit of imagining an alternate scenario. By posing such 'imagine if' questions . . . we can distance ourselves from the frames, cues, anchors and rhetoric that might be affecting us."

—NOREENA HERTZ

"Business has only two functions—marketing and innovation."

—MILAN KUNDERA

CONTENTS

PART III: THE BUILDING BLOCKS OF
DISRUPTIVE MARKETING

PART IV: FOUR SKILLS FOR
THE DISRUPTIVE MARKETER

APPENDICES

FOREWORD

by Gemma Craven,
Senior Vice President, Director of Social and Mobile, McCann Erickson

DID YOU CHOOSE this book because you thought the cover looked interesting? Are you reading this because you have an insatiable curiosity, or because a friend told you about it? Do you see yourself as someone who is in the company of adventurers, visionaries, risk-takers, pioneers, or artists? Are you trying to make sense of a new role, company, industry, or technology, or are you feeling left behind in an era of rapid change?

Whatever your reason for choosing *Disruptive Marketing*, you just made a wise choice. Because in reading this book you have ensured your career will withstand one of the greatest periods of change since the industrial revolution.

Geoffrey and I worked together at Ogilvy & Mather at a time when brand marketers were starting to understand the potential of the new people-fueled online world—a now global mix of platforms, technologies, people, and interest groups we know as the social media. We spent time thinking about new ideas and concepts to bring to clients and colleagues, educating those around us on the potential of how people were behaving in these new digital spaces and tinkering around with new platforms to see how they could work for brands. I was delighted when I read this book: it reminded me of the conversations we had when recording our weekly podcast, but mostly it was the book I always hoped Geoffrey would write.

Geoffrey has always been a gifted storyteller, one with both eyes firmly on the future. He has the ability to take a macro view on the trends and behaviors around and in front of him, in on- and offline worlds, and distill them into a crisp vision for today's marketer.

Disruptive Marketing does just that.

Packed full of ideas you will have a hard time getting out of your head and that you will want to share with those around you, this important book documents the huge change we have seen over the past two decades with the advances in technology, communications, and how they have impacted our lives—and it prepares you, the reader, for the second and third acts to come.

Geoffrey turns to the worlds of sport, punk rock, DJing, teaching, and parenting; he shares anecdotes from history, his varied life experiences, and personal and professional journeys, rather than the somewhat overused case studies of the business book world. This mix shows us exactly what a disruptive marketer is, and while there is no set path to getting there, the behaviors we can all adopt to become one. He challenges us to ask "What if?," demonstrating the huge importance of the question, while painting an exciting picture of how digital marketing is evolving and may well work in the very near future.

Do note: this is not an instruction manual, a step-by-step tutorial, or a guide on the ins and outs of the latest social and digital platforms. This is a foundational text that will change behavior from the linear marketing techniques created in the Don Draper era, to a much more dynamic and fluid approach required for marketing on- and offline, to set us all up for work now and way into the future.

The new workplace is creatively fueled. In commerce, disruption has become the norm. So the disruptive marketer must be both an analytical, creative hybrid and an expert able to deliver across both strategy and execution.

Ditch the reliance on an MBA and pick up this provocative and enlightening read.

Crammed full of tools, theory, relatable reference points and anecdotes, fresh thought leadership, and a superb tour through the tech-fueled world we are living in today, *Disruptive Marketing* is the conspiratorial whisper everyone in business needs to listen to.

Thank you, Geoffrey.

PREFACE

DISRUPTIVE MARKETING WAS written by someone who is curious about and fascinated with how business, human behavior, technology, and communications intersect, and how they are shaped by the world around us. I am a nonconventional marketer because I am unconventional by nature. I love B2B marketing and empowering businesses to think beyond the ordinary. If you ever meet me or get an opportunity to hear me speak, you might think I was an artist, a painter, designer, DJ, or drummer in a rock band—not someone who often wears a suit while trying to sell marketing solutions. But you wouldn't be too far off, either—I have been all of these at different times in my life.

Geoffrey Colon
@djgeoffe

There is no such thing anymore as brand marketing. Customers own your brand. It's customer marketing. #disruptivefm

6:22 PM—21 Feb 2016

My fascination with business disruption is based on my up-bringing and career trajectory. I grew up in Bethlehem, Pennsylvania. For those who haven't heard of it, for many decades it was home to a pretty big business called Bethlehem Steel. When my late father, Frank, moved to Bethlehem from Pittsburgh in 1964, Bethlehem Steel was a $575 million a year enterprise. By the time he approached retirement around the year 2003, the company was gone.

Many say that the issues leading to Bethlehem Steel's demise involved a number of factors, including labor costs, pension costs for its retirees, the price of steel, and decreased demand for industrial steel. Yet, what Bethlehem Steel ignored in the 1980s and 1990s while it toiled in reorganization battles was that specialty steel manufacturers, or "mini-mills," were producing steel at a lower cost. In some respects, Bethlehem Steel was disrupted because it didn't adapt its thinking and processes to the needs of its customers—a common tale in disruptive innovation.

In 1998, while living in New York City and working in the music industry, I read an article in *Music Week* about a technology called MP3. This was at the peak of physically distributed music products. Millions of compact discs by top artists were shipped to customers weekly, to the tune of $15 billion annually.

That *Music Week* article heralded the beginning of the end. Coincidentally, the top-grossing film in 1998 was *Titanic*. You couldn't pick a better metaphor for what was about to occur. Napster dawned in 1999, and solved a problem that the record labels had failed to address. In its most elementary form, Napster was a music discovery sharing service. Sure, people were downloading songs they had no intention of buying, but that's partly because the music industry forced customers to purchase a $17.99 CD with eleven bad songs in order to get the one good single. It was Mafioso Tactics 101 by shrewd business moguls who had learned their trade in the streets and clubs of New York City. Who cares about the end product? Their attitude was, "As long as the spreadsheets don't have any parentheses around the numbers, that's all that matters."

The industry—slow to understand customer sentiment—treated fans like an automatic bank deposit instead of its lifeblood, and became the enemy when it sued Napster in an attempt to halt the behavior.

It was too late. Like most "sue innovation," or what I've dubbed "Californication," movements show us, it's impossible to sue away behavior once it's embedded in people's consciousness. The consumer won, toppling the industry in which I thrived from 1996 to 2002. Later, a guy by the name of Steve Jobs, who started and ran this company called Apple, used the Napster model to usher in iTunes, which became the common and acceptable way to purchase music.

Fast-forward to 2013. I was immersed in the world of the advertising agency. While analyzing some large sets of customer-experience data for one particular project, I noticed that the math didn't add up. Agencies and clients were doing things that were directly at odds with customer behavior. It had been known for some time—and more recently noted in Mary Meeker's 2015 *Internet Trends Report*—that people in the United States spend around one-third of their daily screen time interacting with television and two-thirds with digital media like smartphones. Yet agencies and brands were investing a mere 8 percent of their ad spending on mobile devices, with a much larger allotment (around 41 percent) on television. While television ads allow storytelling in the form of a thirty- or sixty-second spot, the industry was ignoring the fact that user behavior was trending toward an entirely different medium!

Agencies, many of which were built around the TV-industrial advertising complex and billed their time much like law firms to generate revenue, did what most industries do when faced with disruption: instead of being curious and trying to learn new things, they clung to the only way they knew how to keep billings rolling into bank accounts. In economic terms, they tightened the reins of scarcity. They failed to pivot their model, which would have meant doing things very differently from how they had operated for several decades. Many of the top leaders at these agencies simply blamed the radical shifts in customer behavior on "bad data," rather than trying to find new and unique solutions.

The pivot for many disruptive marketers as we near the end of the second decade of the twenty-first century is to take our trade in-house. Seeing the writing on the wall (or the lack thereof) for the decaying agency model, in 2013 I jumped on a cross-country flight to Seattle, where Microsoft waited. This environment is the most interesting in my career to date (in the tech industry, no one is ever safe).

If you enjoy uncertainty, join a tech company or startup. There are no guarantees of success because the business models are built on cognitive capital and imaginary products that come to life via code. In fact, tech companies are probably less safe than others from disruption if they approach business plans with a conventional mindset.

In twentieth-century businesses, the past usually informed a future or ongoing strategy that allowed marketing and management specialists to command the helm. But in the twenty-first century, a business's future success will be designed more than replicated.

The best minds are already doing this: data punks, designers, and creative hybrids, who are more likely to have backgrounds and skills in design, video production, psychology, and statistics, use social business models and insights instead of hierarchical org charts, while immersing themselves in the customer experience and creating culture.

This is disruptive marketing. This is the new normal.

■ ■ ■

I never wear ties at work. They stifle creativity. (I learned this from Richard Branson, who owned a company I had the pleasure of working for from 1999 to 2002.) I don't sit at a desk at Microsoft. Marketing is best performed by getting out in the world and observing things around you; that's because marketing is about people, not faceless data.

I love buying and reading physical books (and though I also love digital, the best way to create digital word of mouth is *post-digital,* which I write about in chapter 8). My background doesn't resemble the traditional path many take to get into the field of marketing.

And I hope after you read more of this book, you will begin to move away from such linear career trajectories, marketing plans, and inefficient organizational hierarchies.

Some of today's best marketing minds don't come from the world of marketing. Many don't have MBAs. To be very successful in this new world, you don't need to follow that path.

In writing this book I didn't want you, the reader, to find it irrelevant if, for example, you don't work for a big company, as I do. (I don't like it when business writers neglect to personalize their books for their readers' diverse backgrounds.) And I don't want you to think this book is only for marketers. While the vast majority of marketers will find the information relevant and, I hope, inspiring, I believe that everyone should read this book to adopt and possess the hacker personality and emotional intelligence required to succeed in business.

As an outsider and culture jammer who now works for a Fortune 500 technology company, it makes little sense to write a book about how MBAs approach marketing with "top of the funnel" models, customer journeys, and value propositions. While there is value in that for some who want the "multiple-choice test," my approach is more like a "blue book" exam. I'll leave the rigid answers to questions of customer segmentation, customer journeys, funnels, and the science of the customer to conventional marketing books written by conventional marketing gurus.

To really enjoy and apply this book to your everyday life I want you to practice something you (not to mention your manager) may think is anathema to the world of work: take twenty minutes a day to *not* look at anything on your phone, computer, or even in the physical world that could distract you. Go on what some call the "digital detox." While you're unplugged, your thoughts should roam as freely as possible and not be cohesive. Imagine anything you want, but remember to ask yourself, "What if?" And also remember to tell yourself, "If only . . ."

Calling on the practice of everyday imaginative thought puts counterfactual thinking to great use. This means thinking of ideas that are clearly not based on data, facts, or reality. Imagine what it might be like to walk upside down for a day, and ask yourself what the advantage would be from that view. Or walk outside and close your eyes and pick a random color. When you open your eyes, try to find as many of those colors as you can in the real world. Or sample my favorite game I play with my two daughters: Create a random animal and give it a name. Then ask yourself, What would that animal do? What would it eat? Where and how would it sleep?

Better yet (and I do this quite a bit), put yourself in the shoes of someone not like yourself at all. If you're a white male who lives in San Francisco, be a black female in Lagos, Nigeria. What does she see, sense, and feel? What would she do for a living? What technology would she be using? What systemic obstacles might she face in her life? This can be powerful and make you realize how innate biases stay rooted in our culture.

Such exercises are important because the power of imagination and empathy is more critical in the world than ever before. As a result, it is even more necessary for people to pay attention to their thoughts, beliefs, actions, and experiences. No thought, debate, or dream is a waste anymore. There is a massive amount of power in being enthusiastically inefficient.

DISRUPTIVE
MARKETING

INTRODUCTION
WHAT IF?

Adventure may hurt, but monotony will kill you.

—AUTHOR UNKNOWN

WHAT IF? THAT is the question you need to ask and answer—multiple times every single day. The solution to every problem begins with this question.

The best marketers don't ask either/or questions. They don't seek answers to questions such as: "Transactions or relationships?" "High touch or high tech?" "Purpose or profit?" "Size or speed?" There is no doubt that we all must make difficult choices in executing brand strategy. But it's no longer about giving up something that is important to you and your customers. In many cases, asking "What if?" helps you find new ways to navigate an ill-defined obstacle course.

TOUGH MUDDER:
AN OBSTACLE COURSE FOR DECISION MAKING

What if I asked you to run through the woods on a muddy trail with me? That's exactly what my co worker Laurel Geisbush asked me to do in 2013 when I arrived at Microsoft. But this wasn't your average mud run. This was an obstacle and endurance course created by two Harvard Business School students, Guy Livingstone and Will Dean. Its name? Tough Mudder.

Tough Mudder is a great analogy for the world we occupy as marketers. The demanding physical course features several decision-making scenarios requiring the traverser to work creatively and collaboratively to be successful. To the unacquainted, the obstacle course can be a mare's nest of irrational decision making, whether there is one leader everyone follows or if everyone attempts the course on his or her own. That's the point. What the organizers want you to do is to make decisions—many of them uncomfortable—quickly and spontaneously.

In Tough Mudder, groups that think obstacles through "on the fly" benefit from using a "What if" rather than an "Either/or" decision-making process, although several of the obstacles require a straight linear-thought trajectory.

The Biggest Obstacle: Consumers in Control

Shaping business around real customer behavior is the challenge facing us as marketers today. It's our version of Tough Mudder. Unfortunately, companies are still built and structured to solve linear, twentieth-century marketing issues. The marketing skills that used to work splendidly are incompatible with today's world.

Phillipa Reed, director at Think Big Social, in London, defined the current situation brilliantly when she wrote about brands in a thought-leadership piece for LinkedIn: "There is an increasing trend away from consumers simply being influenced by brands, to the point where brands are now increasingly being controlled and influenced by their consumers."

The primary driver of this distinct trend is the influence that social networks, smartphones, apps, online forums, and blogs have had on how we live our lives. The continuing takeover by digital media has ushered in the reimagination of the roles once controlled by brand strategists, media buyers, advertising agencies, brands, and marketing departments. While customers were once subject to the whim of brand messages, they now can act as media creators, publishers, producers, and critics. In other words, brands have less control than ever before and must be willing to adapt to this newfound reality.

Ask yourself:

- What if we developed messages as marketers that had nothing to do with stories, but more to do with social responsibility?
- What if we decided to ditch all the ways we as marketers have tried to improve brand perception via impression-based metrics and instead looked to other metrics such as sentiment as a guide for our efforts?
- What if we disrupt revenue models gained from conventional practices like media buying and advertising for more nonconventional practices like customer relationship management (CRM) and customer design and development of new products?

Sounds easy and dangerous at the same time, doesn't it? Well, for some of you it may be too dangerous, which is one reason marketing is stagnating. In my opinion, mainstream marketing is not changing to reflect rapidly evolving customer behavior.

The Biggest Problem: Sticking to the Old Ways of Solving Problems

One of the biggest problems in business is the unwillingness to come up with new ways to creatively solve problems. In the agency world where I spent most of my career, people are always trying to solve problems. Customer-experience problems, client problems, design problems, technology problems. Yet, most work in the twenty-first century will revolve around problem solving. Why? Because the world is complex. We face a number of hurdles that non-imaginative and non-people-centric problem-solving models will have a hard time addressing.

Too many businesses treat customer problems as employee problems. Because employees are not able to solve a customer's problem, they blame it on the employee's incompetence, instead of looking for new solutions. They are unwilling to try different things to solve the customer's issues. And the cycle goes on and on.

Why is that? I believe that in part it's the consultants to whom businesses turn for answers. Most business books, for example, are written by professionals who hide behind their MBA or 30 years of experience as if they were badges of honor, when in fact the indicators of success that we used to take for granted are now irrelevant, thanks to data and indirect knowledge. As a result, books and blogs with rigidly defined, step-by-step, linear solutions may seem helpful but can actually be harmful in the real business world. Their assumptions are incorrect because they are centered on methodology and technology, not on people.

Solving problems by asking the "What if" question is more helpful because it takes people into consideration rather than simply following a set of pre established resolution blueprints. For every problem you are trying to solve, you should be asking more questions. The Socratic method is as popular as ever in a liberal arts education because it helps develop critical thinking skills that are so needed in the business world—including marketing—for the twenty-first century.

CASE IN POINT
Looking for Answers

Think of the question I'm about to ask as one presented in an agency creative brief. For purposes of this discussion, I'm the client presenting a set of problems or issues to which you, the agency, will help provide solutions.

Let's set the context. You work for a midsize international company, on their marketing team based in Mumbai, India. Your company is about to ship a new product to go to market. Where do you start your marketing plan? In other words, is there a correct or regimented way for planning and executing your marketing strategy? Do you start by listing a set of tactics? Do you follow a linear, step-by-step process model? Or, do you see things others cannot? (I don't mean that you see dead people, although M. Night Shyamalan did get the idea for his groundbreaking film *The Sixth Sense* from a Nickelodeon show.) For example, do you see what industries outside your own are doing, ↓

and are you influenced by them to find new ways to solve marketing problems?

Do you answer this question by telling me that you will sit down with a few other marketers and salespeople and draft a plan in a Power-Point deck that includes your value proposition and ways to generate customer demand? Or, are you a more freewheeling marketer who puts a few thoughts and a timeline in a Word document and has an idea in your head of how the messaging you create and develop will land and who it is gauged to influence? Do you write a press release for the product to judge how it will be perceived and poke holes in it so that you can reshape it to define the message?

According to *Fast Company* magazine, this is actually something that Amazon's Jeff Bezos makes his teams do when they are about to launch a new product idea. Or, using mobile communication tools like Slack, do you roll up your sleeves and begin to iterate, with no prepared plan of action or strategy, in real time? What if I asked you which is more important: your product, your strategy, or your marketing plan execution? What if I asked who your target customer is for this new product? Could you answer that question truthfully? Or would your answer be your *desired* audience rather than one rooted in factual data?

What if I told you that no matter how you answered any of my queries, you are incorrect? That there is no single, defined correct answer—no one-size-fits-all solution—to any of the questions I asked. What if I told you I purposely left out a few answers to see if you came up with anything outside the box? What if I told you that the reason I asked you this question in the first place was to see if you worked toward a defined and rigid answer like a business school project or came up with a number of high-level solutions like a startup data scientist? What if I told you that a defined and rigid answer, even if it was "correct" on paper, would not be the correct answer for the purpose of this quiz? What if I told you that any defined and rigid answer to these questions would be incorrect because it showcases a conventional-thinking personality trait?

Think back to the multiple-choice math tests you took when you were in grade school. You had to choose only one answer, and you were rewarded for your correct answers with a passing grade. Now fast-forward to high school or college. Do you remember taking a class in which the teacher asked you one question and told you to fill a blue book with your answer? It was complicated, wasn't it? The solution wasn't always well defined. There were intricacies and possibilities that could be applied depending on the scenario.

Geoffrey Colon
@djgeoffe

What if we approached marketing like we treat computer code? #disruptivefm

6:23 PM—21 Feb 2016

What if I told you that computer programmers are not all nerds, outcasts, or misogynistic *brogrammers*; that I know and work on a daily basis with especially smart and creative women; that all marketers are not alike; that it's a diverse field and many are adventurers, visionaries, risk-takers, pioneers, and artists?

CODE: IT'S NOT JUST FOR NERDS

Many of us are biased in thinking that computer programmers are a bunch of backroom geeks who don't step outside the rigid confines of defined languages and stereotypes. But if computer programmers lived in a vacuum, would we have all the unique and innovative applications many of us use to conduct more productive lives?

Back in 2011, when I joined Ogilvy & Mather as a vice president of digital strategy, I learned a minimal amount about how to code. In 2009, my old agency colleague Dominic Basulto, who currently is the innovation blogger for the *Washington Post*, said it would be important for everyone, whether in tech or teaching, in the military or working for a nonprofit, to learn code.

Code, he said, is the language of the future, enabling us to "make things." I took his advice, and when my oldest daughter was around two years old, I started a Ruby on Rails class at codeacademy.com. I wanted to go beyond being simply a thinker and become a maker. While learning code, I realized that in the twenty-first century, programming and marketing are both creative and mechanical exercises and are more alike than many of us are led to believe.

People unfamiliar with coding think you just follow simple rules and, boom, you have a solution or an app, that magically works on your iPhone or Surface tablet or Chromebook. The same can be said about marketing. That sentence I used to describe programmers? Let me recite it again: *Adventurers, visionaries, risk-takers, pioneers, and artists.* Yet that description doesn't simply apply to the average computer programmer; it also applies to a segment of outcasts and outsider marketers: data punks, designers, and creative hybrids.

This segment can't be defined by their marketing roles because they can do it all: crunch code, write stories, and produce and distribute video content using paid search and social media. Some call them growth hackers. I call them disruptive marketers.

ADAPT OR DIE

The analogy that may best explain business in the twenty-first century is biology, the study of life and living organisms, including their growth and evolution. Think of business as a living, breathing animal. How it adapts or fails to adapt is a major determiner of its survival.

With that in mind, let's return to my original question. What if we had some data about the fictitious new product that our company was about to ship, and I said: "Don't tell me who the target audience is. Instead, pull a piece of data that contradicts your normal view of the world and then tell me how the product *could* be marketed based on that unique data."

Quick, think back to what I just said about tests. This isn't a multiple-choice quiz, is it? No, this is a blue book examination.

Geoffrey Colon
@djgeoffe

Disruptive marketing is more of a blue book exam than multiple-choice. #disruptivefm

6:24 PM—21 Feb 2016

DISRUPTIVE MARKETING

- Allows you to see things others cannot because they can't separate themselves from their innate biases—that is, what they perceive as "the right kind of marketing" and what might be unchartered territory as defined by the data.
- Makes it okay for you to be curious, to daydream, to be enthusiastically inefficient, and to allow your mind to wander and tinker with inconvenient facts.
- Is about not following the rules of conventional marketing but, rather, establishing your own rules because the new norms of the creative economy demand it.
- Questions everything you learned from primary school to business school because linear patterns don't make up the real world we inhabit or the one we must create as a result of technology-inspired behavior.
- Does not explain away data-centricities with excuses like "bad batch of data," "small sample size," "not enough data," and "that's not our target audience because I have an innate bias that it shouldn't be."
- Understands the allure of conventional marketing and the challenge of leaving it behind to forge a new path using disruptive thinking and actions. But the latter can unlock opportunities usually hidden right in front of us that the former is reluctant to identify.
- Is for those who inspired it: data punks, designers, creative hybrids, growth hackers, bandits, delinquents, and business rebels of all shapes and sizes who will reconfirm your

knowledge so you can help bring it to others in your organization, whatever the objectives (tech products, consumer packaged goods, industrial design products, innovative ideas, politics, new ways of thinking, philosophies) and whatever you would like to apply it to.

- Helps empower everyone through a rapid and radical time of business turbulence, when if you don't lead the change and transformation, others—in this case your customers—will lead it for you.
- Rewards those who find and seek new opportunities in creative ways because they have more diligence than intelligence.
- Helps overcome preconceived ideas about what makes marketing work by testing and trying things that are smaller, subtler, and more immersive yet more effective than million-dollar campaigns by big companies like Nike and Coca-Cola.
- Is for thinkers, doers, questioners, and subversive naysayers who realize the most lethal phrase in business is, "But we've always done it this way."
- Doesn't necessarily have to be related to revenue. In fact, you'll read later in this book why revenue is a poor target for survival.

THE DE-DON DRAPERIZATION OF MARKETING

What exactly does this new world look like? Well, it is a converged world full of large and tiny touch screens, data as insight, people yearning for experiences and meaning rather than consuming things, and an emerging "do it yourself" collaborative and remixed economy powered by user-generated content, production, design, and feelings, with a heavy emphasis on a company's reputation and culture instead of monetary capital. In other words, everything you've come to learn about what makes efficient or successful marketing is actually inefficient and incorrect.

Geoffrey Colon

@djgeoffe

The amount of marketing experience one has means little in a world constantly changing via design. #disruptivefm

6:24 PM—21 Feb 2016

Marketing today doesn't look very different from how it has for the last half century, nor has it truly disrupted itself inside and out mainly because of the attitude of marketers and advertising agencies. No industry disrupts itself. That's why it's important we look at how people other than those who call themselves marketers behave. I've had the pleasure of interviewing several of them for this book and what they have to say will help you prepare for the new normal.

Advertising agencies are also difficult to trust for innovative answers or solutions because, in wanting to stay the course that had historically made money rather than charting a new future, they made the biggest mistake in modern business: they defended themselves instead of going forth and conquering. As a result, agencies blew four opportunities to remain relevant:

1. They missed the digital train. They ignored the dotcom industry, thinking it would go bust.
2. They ignored search engines because they didn't ask "What if" questions about where the world could be headed with smartphones and location-based technology.
3. They ignored social media marketing because they thought people would only use search engines and platforms such as Facebook, Twitter, and LinkedIn wouldn't ever be as big as the "big media" of cable and network television.
4. They were late to the content-marketing game because they didn't understand why people used the social web and Internet in the first place. It was hardly to make friends with brands; it really was a place to connect and learn.

Agencies missed these four trends and will continue to miss many more because of the group-think and conformity embedded in their DNA.

What agencies failed to realize is that marketing is more than messaging. It's more than advertising. It's more than broadcasting. It's more than simply return on investment (ROI). Agencies also failed to realize that marketing isn't devoid of math anymore. Nor should math reduce creativity to a Post-it note on a social platform instructing visitors to "read more," "learn more," "download more," or "watch more." People aren't responsive to what sounds like commands from a military general.

If anything, math makes marketing more creative, not less. Marketing in a disruptive sense is the way we all can and should use data to build more meaningful products, create alliances to solve the world's most daunting problems, get people to adopt new ways of thinking, solve customer problems, and rethink how business and possibly the economy will operate differently in the next decade.

Even David Ogilvy, one of the godfathers of advertising and the inspiration for Don Draper's character in the cable television show *Mad Men*, knew that data would be more relevant than creative efforts alone. Ogilvy was as much a futurist in this area as anyone else. To me, he was one of the first disruptive marketers. It's a shame his beliefs don't resonate in our world as much as they should. When reading the following passage, replace Ogilvy's phrase "direct response" with "disruptive marketing":

In the advertising community today there are two worlds. Your world of direct response advertising and that other world, that world of general advertising. These two worlds are on a collision course. You direct response people know what kind of advertising works and what doesn't work. You know to a dollar. The general advertising people don't know. You know that two-minute commercials on television are more effective, more cost-effective than 10-second commercials or 30-second commercials. You know that fringe time on television sells more than prime time. In print advertising, you know that long copy sells more than short copy. You know that headlines and copy about the product and its benefits sell more than cute headlines and poetic copy. You know to a dollar. The general advertisers and their agencies know almost nothing for sure because they cannot measure the results of their advertising. They worship at the altar of creativity. Which really means originality. The most dangerous word in the lexicon of advertising. They opine that 30-second commercials are more cost-effective than two-minute commercials. You know they're wrong. In print advertising, they opine that short commercials sell more than long copy. You know they're wrong. They indulge in entertainment. You know they're wrong. You know to a dollar. They don't. Why don't you tell them? Why don't you save them from their follies? For two reasons. First, because you're impressed by the fact that they're so big and so well paid and so well publicized. You're even perhaps impressed by their reputation for creativity, whatever that may mean. Second, you never meet them. You've inhabited different worlds. The chasm between direct response advertising and general advertising is wide. On your side of the chasm I see knowledge and reality. On the other side of the chasm I see ignorance. You are the professionals. This must not go on. I predict that the practitioners of general advertising are going to start learning from your experience. They are going to start picking your brains.

Geoffrey Colon

@djgeoffe

Marketing to generate solely revenue and profit is so 20th century. #disruptivefm

6:24 PM — 21 Feb 2016

Sadly and incorrectly, marketing is something many businesses compartmentalize into silos.

The Solution: Stop Treating Marketing like a Silo Operation

Marketing is still seen as its own organization that takes products, services, solutions, or messages to market using gut-level instincts. Traditionally, marketing has been viewed as a group of people with glamorous job titles like managing director, senior vice president, vice president, director, manager, and coordinator whose main functions are to lead the horse to the water in the hope that it will drink.

This, of course, is a conventional, twentieth-century way of viewing marketing roles. With software and data analytics, marketing can now be more of a creative workshop to build new products based on customer experience. While software may be disrupting how marketing functions, it is also flipping the table on how organizations assemble products and go-to-market strategies, even reorganizing teams where creative hybrids apply real-time, data-driven decision making.

As the global economy evolves and market forces drive competition for jobs, including marketing roles, people who have proactively worked to expand and diversify their skill sets will be the most well placed in the creative economy. When you synthesize your knowledge and skills into a new offering, you evolve from a knowledge economy worker into a creative economy entrepreneur. Thomas Friedman wrote about just this scenario in his book *The World Is Flat*: "Everyone is looking for employees who can do critical thinking and problem solving. . . . What they are really looking for are people who can invent, re-invent and re-engineer their jobs while doing them."

Conventional marketers and advertisers may be satisfied that they are still generating revenue right now. The question isn't a matter of if but when that all will come to a fizzled end. Vivek Wadwha, a fellow at Rock Center for Corporate Governance, at Stanford University; director of research at the Center for Entrepreneurship and Research Commercialization at Duke University; and distinguished fellow at the think-tank/university Singularity University in California, wrote a December 2014 *Washington Post* article about this. His message should make conventional marketers raise their eyes from the email they spend too much time sending and take notice that not only will the marketing industry be disrupted but every industry in which marketing has a role, from manufacturing to supply-chain management, from finance to energy, and from health care to education to communications, will also be disrupted.

According to Wadwha, not one industry is immune from the rapid change that is about to dismantle everything we've become accustomed to. Wadwha wrote:

> In practically every industry that I look at, I see a major disruption happening. I know the world will be very different 15 to 20 years from now. The vast majority of companies who are presently the leaders in their industries will likely not even exist. That is because industry executives are either not aware of the changes that are coming, reluctant to invest the type of money required for them to reinvent themselves, or protecting legacy businesses. Most are focused on short-term performance. New trillion-dollar industries will come out of nowhere and wipe out existing trillion-dollar industries. This is the future we're headed into, for better or for worse.

The type of disruption Wadwha was talking about isn't new. First, we moved from an agricultural era to an industrial era, then to a knowledge era, and now to a new creative age. People who find opportunities in a changing environment are those who are actively looking for them. Marketers included.

Marketing now allows for new ways to initiate small-batch creative execution. Today you can analyze data on how people interact with the messaging or experience, monitor what they actually say about your company, test reactions to new features, and work in conjunction with your customers to build better products or a better world.

Marketing isn't just for businesses, either. Nor is it something done only by the marketing department or by people with "marketing" in their title. Marketing can and should be used by nonprofits, governments, politicians, scientists, and anyone else who deals with spreading and adopting new ideas.

MARKETING AND THE NEW NORMAL

The creative imagination is important because right before our very eyes we are transitioning to what Peter Drucker called a "post-capitalist economy." It scares many people who cannot see beyond the standard of living to which many of us have become accustomed.

Cognitive capitalism has begun to rapidly erode the industrial economy. Marketing still rooted in that industrial economy has no choice but to go in a different direction. Hence, talking about marketing ideas or products without discussing the overall shift in the economy would make this book irrelevant. Tactics and techniques don't live on islands, unto themselves. They are part of the larger world around us.

Those who approach this book with both feet firmly rooted in the twentieth century will have a hard time understanding some of the tools and personality traits required to make the leap. Even if you work in an industrial-era company that includes manufacturing or producing tangible goods, you'll find that all companies will become social by design in the next five years.

The best companies and organizations will act and think very much like open-source software. Success will be determined by constantly testing and experimenting with new designs. Design is at the center of all human experience.

Steve Jobs built Apple—which as of this writing is the world's most valuable company—by focusing not on technology or marketing but on design. While I am a huge fan of engineering degrees and engineers (I did go to Lehigh University, a school heavily rooted in engineering), I believe that empathy, design, and emotional intelligence—three key skills for disruptive marketing and design—are better learned from an immersion in the arts, humanities, and psychology than from pure business, engineering, and management disciplines. An art history major who has studied paintings of the impressionists or "outsider art" may have gained insights into the human elements of technology and the importance of its usability. Psychologists and sociologists are more likely than pure marketers to know how to motivate people and understand what users want. A musician, chef, or fine artist who is driven to create always leads and innovates in a world in which we can develop almost anything we imagine.

The most disruptive marketers believe in using all possibilities available to them, including nondigital tools, in a world with ever more abundant goods and greater access to ever more information. This sometimes runs in contradiction to older systems rooted in hierarchy, monopoly, and scarcity. However, those who look for networks, platforms, and hive mind thinking to be the new avenues of feedback engagement and growth will find success.

In a world where authenticity and transparency reign supreme, marketing rooted in scarcity will have a short shelf life. Business schools have taught many to think that the 4Ps (product, price, promotion, place) are guarantees of success. In 2012, the 4Ps were updated to pivot toward people, processes, programs, and performance, but even this is becoming antiquated thinking in a world where process is redefined almost hourly based on customer behavior. The descriptions of the skills many say a marketer should possess are usually off the mark now in a matter of months, not years, because of advances in technology and customer behavior that adapt to those changes more rapidly than do businesses.

David Zweig, author of *Invisibles: Celebrating the Unsung Heroes of the Workplace*, declares that what brand marketers have been taught in terms of framing, identity, and promotion is now highly irrelevant:

> So, aside from the time invested/wasted in promoting yourself online, and thinking about how to promote yourself, that could likely be better spent actually working on whatever it is you do, creating stuff, rather than marketing yourself as someone who creates stuff, there's now the real risk of alienating the people you are trying to impress. . . .
>
> Because it's become so pervasive, there's a growing sense that when someone is branding or promoting themselves too much or in too overt a way, that they are dishonest. Because after all, branding, if not inherently dishonest, certainly is about only promoting the positive. . . . Even if the brand you create is accurate, and not purposefully intended as a promotional lie, the problem still is the fact that you are spending too much time worrying about how you appear to others.

If you have this promotional mindset, you'll want to relearn what you've been taught, based on Zweig's points. Having marketing skills and an MBA is no longer enough to be successful. Being a promotional zealot will make you appear dishonest, even if what you are saying is the truth. None of what you've been taught about marketing will give you enough leverage in a world filled with abundant ideas, solutions, products, data, and services.

Disruptive marketers understand that technology dictates the pace of change in human behavior, and that technology's evolution is accelerating at an exponential rate. This is known as Moore's Law, which states that over the history of computing hardware, the number of transistors in a dense integrated circuit has doubled approximately every two years. In a 1965 paper, Gordon E. Moore, co-founder of Intel Corporation and Fairchild Semiconductor, described a yearly doubling in the number of components per integrated circuit. In 1975, he altered the forecast, revising that time to every two years. Moore's Law is used in the semiconductor industry to guide long-term planning and to set targets for research and development. The capabilities of many digital electronic devices are strongly linked to Moore's Law: quality-adjusted microprocessor prices, memory capacity, sensors, and even the number and size of pixels in digital cameras. All of these are improving at roughly exponential rates as well.

DESIGNING DISRUPTION

Where did the concept of disruptive marketing originate and why do I use it? It's rooted in the terms *creative disruption* and *disruptive innovation*. Creative disruption is doing things in the creative process differently from before. Disruptive innovation is an advance that helps create a new market that eventually (over a few years or decades) overthrows or topples an existing market, displacing an earlier technology.

There are many examples of disruptive innovation in the history of technology: the transistor radio (which displaced high-fidelity players), mini steel mills (which displaced vertically integrated steel mills), ultrasound (which displaced radiography), downloadable digital media (which displaced physical products like CDs and DVDs), and Wikipedia (which displaced printed encyclopedias).When we talk about disruptive marketing, we mean the act of *designing* brand strategy differently from how it was previously created.

PART I
A WORLD WITHOUT RULES

CHAPTER 1
THE DISRUPTIVE MINDSET
Create, Engage, Adapt

The true scarce commodity is increasingly human attention.
— SATYA NADELLA,
Chief Executive Officer, Microsoft

ONE HOT AND humid evening in late August 1922 a sound wave coursed through the New York City sky. Only those with a radio console tuned to 660 AM could hear the male voice, speaking in a "you'd-better-not-miss-this" tone, which traveled those airwaves.

The station was not WFAN Sports Radio, "The FAN," which currently inhabits that frequency, where on-air hosts spend hours talking about the failures of the Jets and the Knicks. This station, whose call letters were WEAF, pumped out a steady stream of talk, news, and cultural tidbits interspersed with jazz and swing—the popular music of the early 1920s. Who could have guessed that the one male voice, speaking nonstop for about sixty seconds at 5 PM on that August evening, would ultimately transform how electronic communications would operate for the next eighty years.

> Friend, you owe it to yourself and your family to leave the congested city and enjoy what nature intended you to enjoy. Visit our new apartment homes in Hawthorne Court, Jackson Heights, where you may enjoy community life in a friendly environment.

Today, Jackson Heights is a densely populated area that pulses with the captivating odors of Colombian, Ecuadorian, and Argentinean cuisine punctuated by street-corner discussions on *fútbol* clubs like Deportivo Cali, Emelec, and Boca Juniors. In 1922, however, this part of Queens was still being developed and that early radio ad touted its virtues.

In the modern era, anyone who still listens to AM/FM radio anywhere in the world will find an on-air commercial like this commonplace. But in 1922, it was new. Why would a voice bark out a message about the Hawthorne Court Apartments? Was it part of the evening's programming? Or was something else behind it?

What listeners at the time did not know was that Hawthorne Court had shelled out $50, the modern-day equivalent of $678.64, factoring for inflation, to WEAF. Essentially what listeners heard that evening was the first paid radio advertisement.

Of course we understand that ads or content like this doesn't simply end up on the air naturally. During my daily drive home on the crowded Interstate 405 from Bellevue to Kirkland, Washington, the Ron and Don Show on 97.3 FM KIRO radio will, out of nowhere, say something like, "Hey, do you want to eat a fresh lunch? Subway, eat fresh," before continuing to talk about that day's news. They do it so casually it's as if they hadn't interrupted the flow of the news to promote Subway. But we all know that these on-air personalities didn't simply decide to talk about Subway or any of their favorite eateries without compensation to the station.

Third parties want to use media to reach audiences they feel will use their services or purchase their products. This is pretty common knowledge. The Hawthorne Court Apartments radio advertisement on WEAF was intended to appeal to a middle-class, radio-owning audience. But how did WEAF know to do this? Why did station management decide to take money from the Hawthorne Court Apartments in the first place?

To answer that, we need to look back to those who shaped radio into an advertising channel that would eventually influence its later cousins, television and the Internet. As is often true when something is done differently, it wasn't radio people who developed the idea that led to selling advertising time on the radio. In fact, like most disruptive scenarios, the idea of radio advertising came from a source outside the radio business.

DISRUPTIVE MARKETING AND
THE CREATION OF RADIO ADVERTISING

Actually, the idea for radio advertising came from the telephone industry. Specifically, it was the telephone call, not the telephone hardware, that ushered in the radio advertising model. In 1913, Bell Telephone and its parent, AT&T, unwittingly joined the radio race when it acquired a patent for the vacuum tube, which turned out to play a central role in radio broadcasting. As a result, AT&T had a prominent stake in the radio in 1922 when the station it owned, WEAF, aired that ad. But how did AT&T come up with the concept of selling airtime to third parties? The answer lies in telephone usage and behavior.

In this era, there was no rotary phone. You would pick up the transmitter and an operator would come on the other end of the line and say, "Operator; how may I direct your call?" and you would tell the operator the number, and she would connect the call. The underlying technology of the telephone—that any message could be carried and connected to any place at any time—was the connective link. Once the parties were connected, the operator left, and all the caller would pay for was the length of the call from that moment.

Herein lies the centerpiece of the future commercial broadcasting industry. The mechanics of placing a telephone call today (if you even make a phone call using a landline, with all the available alternatives of email, SMS, text applications, social networks, Slack, WhatsApp, etc.) are camouflaged in the convenience of area codes and direct dialing. But even mobile phone users know that what we are still buying from the AT&Ts, T-Mobiles, and Verizons of the world is time measured in exact minutes and seconds on a communication system for hire.

A Solution out of Thin Air

WEAF essentially was one of the first disruptive marketers. It found an answer to the problem that was in "plain blind sight," also known as "inattentional blindness," which Christopher Chabris and Daniel Simons discuss in their book, *The Invisible Gorilla*.

Thus, WEAF asked a "What if" question that the radio industry needed to solve: "What if we finance an endless stream of programming by giving airtime to businesses who will pay us for it?" This, of course, is an ongoing question for media; think of the freemium applications you download onto your smartphone. But in 1922, AT&T figured out a solution to a problem that others may have seen but hadn't solved: how to bring together space, time, and reach to create a revenue model. This financial structure, used by the marketing industry ever since, is how most media outlets became cash rich in the twentieth century.

In the 1920s, the radio was a consumer item, a piece of furniture housed in an attractive wooden cabinet, with simple controls designed for anyone to operate. Think of it as comparable to today's smartphone. But unlike your smartphone, which monetizes itself via data and calling plans, in 1922 the radio had a lot of time but, seemingly, nothing to sell to pay for the operating costs and technology.

The concept of time as revenue has always been used in economic models. In fact, AT&T was already using that model when, in 1922, it decided to sell what it called "toll broadcasting" on radio. The company simply brought payment for time and access from one technology (telephone) to another (radio). And it worked. Across many industries, time is the essential ingredient in the billing and revenue-generation process.

In fact, if you're reading this during work hours, technically you're going to have to make up that time later in order to earn your income. Even if you don't bill by the hour, time is what your annual salary is based on. And if you work a shift, you are effectively billing a particular rate per hour. This rate is one set by the government, the employer, a combination of the two, or by you if you are offering a service as a third-party vendor.

Time billing is how professionals such as lawyers, consultants, construction people, and even creative services make most of their income. Therefore, it makes sense that time is the essential value that the media sell to third parties who want to use those media to reach audiences. Time is what advertisers are basically paying for when they buy media for their message.

Yet, time isn't the sole quotient in this model.

In 1922, WEAF had a large listening audience because it covered a one-hundred-square-mile radius in a metro area with close to 5.6 million people. Because WEAF owned the technology and could rent that time to third parties that wanted to reach their audiences, we entered an era known as "pay to reach." This was later amplified by television and the Internet, and more recently social media platforms like Facebook. For the remainder of the twentieth century, marketers essentially paid for two things when they bought media on third-party platforms: space and time.

Geoffrey Colon
@djgeoffe

In old media, marketers paid for space and time. In emerging media, marketers will pay for audience and attention. #disruptivefm

6:25 PM – 21 Feb 2016

All of those models of space and time in the form of billboards, newspaper and magazine ads, radio and television spots, digital online banner ads, Facebook ads, promoted tweets, and pre-roll video (the annoying thirty-second video spots you see on YouTube, the ones with the "Skip This Ad" buttons that I know you hurriedly tap) are now seen as distractions and clutter.

WHY ADS DON'T MATTER ANYMORE

We have become accustomed to tuning out the advertising and marketing messages because we don't like interruptions in our habit-formed lives. And we're skeptical of the messages ads bring us. In fact, most of us feel ads don't bring much value to our lives, just more distraction.

There's another reason we tune out ads. Frank Rose, author of *The Art of Immersion: How the Digital Generation Is Remaking Hollywood, Madison Avenue, and the Way We Tell Stories,* explained this to me in a Skype chat. Frank spent many years as a writer at *Wired* magazine. Many of his pieces were on the intersections of media, technology, and human behavior. There is no better person to talk to about this than Frank.

On why ads don't matter as much anymore, Frank said, "The main reason is people are so much more media savvy than they used to be and it's not hard to figure out that advertisers are simply trying to advertise." Frank Rose noted how the power that technology gives to users reshapes their behavior. We can see it in our day-to-day lives. How many of you reading this book watch live television anymore? Do you own a DVR that gives you the capability to fast-forward through the ads? Do you even pay cable companies to access their content from a cable converter box, or are you a cord cutter? How many of you click on the banner ads, search ads, Facebook ads, or *any* other ad on your mobile device?

Rose is right: the world we live in is focused on how we personalize our experiences, which inevitably leads to rapid withdrawal from the interruptive advertising format. As he put it,

> If you look back at the history of marketing, which came about in the mid-century in the 1950s with the rise of mass media, people were not very sophisticated. The whole 1960s approach to marketing is obsolete. . . . People are so much more sophisticated largely because of the Internet. The Internet has called into question the whole thirty-second spot. People had to watch those because they had no choice back in the day. You only had three channels and limited options. People don't want clutter. The whole point of marketing now is moving toward creating messages that people want to share with others.

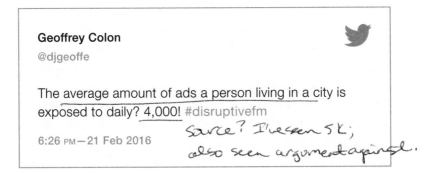

Geoffrey Colon
@djgeoffe

The average amount of ads a person living in a city is exposed to daily? 4,000! #disruptivefm

6:26 PM—21 Feb 2016

[handwritten note: Source? I've seen 5k; also seen argument against.]

Nevertheless, Rose said, organizations aren't systemically ready for disruptive marketing. No matter how many articles you read about digital, social, or mobile marketing in *Advertising Age, Adweek, Digiday,* or some marketing blog, conventional marketing is the norm. And the data backs it up.

In a study, the market research firm eMarketer reports that most big brands still put heavy emphasis on creating thirty-and sixty-second television spots, even though there are many other options that would get more traction. According to that same study, TV ad spending is forecast to be in the $75 billion range by 2017. According to Rose,

> Interruption is something people will try to avoid at all costs and it's not effective for the advertiser. It's a completely different scenario but for some reason many people in business haven't acknowledged this. These are the same people [who] said the Internet [was] a fad during the dotcom era of the early 2000s [and they] still hold power in business. There's that mindset that is prevalent in the residue of the marketing community. To me that is a recipe for failure, but what do you do instead?

What you do instead is exactly what Rose was trying to answer in a program he runs at Columbia University's School of the Arts digital storytelling lab. Rose was quick to point out a trend he identified years ago:

> One thing that is interesting to me is that "storytelling" was not even on many people's lips when I wrote [my] book. If you

think about it, journalists are storytellers. . . . When I worked at *Wired* magazine I wrote about anything and everything [at] . . . the intersection of media and technology. I did a few pieces which led me to realize there are all sorts of people who worked in TV who went to video game companies [and] then went to work in web video. This cross-pollination . . . [among] all three of these industries is what [created] a whole new [way] we interact with others through stories.

Rose's program is at the cutting edge of the new norm, which isn't storytelling, but what he has dubbed the "enchanted state."

THE NEW NORM: THE ENCHANTED STATE

Frank Rose pointed to Brian Boyd, author of *On the Origin of Stories: Evolution, Cognition, and Fiction.* Boyd notes something that many in physics would admire. When the world is noisy, the way to cancel out the noise is actually through additional noise. Not noise at a higher decibel level, but noise at the same level as the original noise, only on a different wavelength. Boyd dubs this technique "the conspiratorial whisper," and he notes, "When everyone is shouting, the way to get people's attention is to whisper."

> **Geoffrey Colon**
> @djgeoffe
>
>
> "When everyone is shouting, the way to get people's attention is to whisper." —Brian Boyd #disruptivefm
>
> 11:40 PM—3 Mar 2016

Frank Rose added,

The current taste for immersion is largely a by-product of the digital age. Video games and the Internet have taught people to be active participants rather than passive observers; just looking is no longer enough. People expect to dive in, and companies as disparate as Disney, Facebook, and Burberry have been scrambling to oblige them. But although digital technology seems to encourage it, immersion can be triggered by almost any form of media, starting with books and theater. People have been immersing themselves in stories for centuries.

This new normal has not been kind to conventional marketers. Many still trust customer journeys, rational decision-making purchase models, inbound marketing tactics (email, search, social), and noisy ads as the biggest drivers for their campaigns. David Zweig notes in his book *Invisibles* that this "noisy world" may originate from the current work ethic, which is rooted in using our brashness to draw attention to ourselves. "We've been taught that the squeaky wheel gets the grease, that to not just get ahead, but to matter, to exist even, we must make ourselves seen and heard."

Rose, too, felt this is the wrong way to approach marketing. He mentioned the radical swing of companies that aren't employing attention-grabbing techniques or tactics. There is a bubbling trend just beginning to make headway in marketing circles. "Some companies let their customers create or string their own stories together," he said. "It makes people feel like they have ownership."

To take it a step further, disruptive marketers are heading up some companies on the radical fringe that go beyond their own creative assets and intellectual property, and allow customers to piece together the stories. In this "enchanted state," the stories may begin to even include competitors' assets so customers can begin to create mashups or bootleg stories.

Yet much of this new paradigm seems beyond the reach of a compartmentalized marketing department conditioned to create a story that allows it to push and control brand narratives and value propositions. This new form of storytelling makes sense. It's classically disruptive in its nature because it derives from the world of tech more than from the world of advertising.

WHAT'S HOLDING MARKETERS BACK
FROM GOING ALL IN?

If I were to ask you to pull out your smartphone right now (or if you're reading this on a tablet or laptop, any connected device you choose) and scan it for the apps you use on a daily basis to work, to live, and to communicate, would all of those apps have been developed by the same company?

Of course not. First, your operating system came installed with certain applications, whether you're using iOS, OSX, Windows 10, or Android. Second, you may use software like OneDrive to back up your photos, but Dropbox to package them and send them to other people. Just as our world is inhabited by information technology professionals, we are our own CTOs (chief technology officers) when it comes to our devices and how we use them to experience the world. If this is true of us, why don't brands do the same and allow their audiences to immerse themselves in a way that may be disruptive and that may include competitors' content?

For this answer, I turned to the "power couple of digital marketing," Rebecca Carlson and Eric Drumm. I've known them for the past decade, as they have toiled as disruptive marketers for a variety of agencies and tech startups, including 360i, Ogilvy, Sprinklr, and FindSpark. Now both have interesting roles on the brand side and in the agency world. Carlson, or "Reb," as she likes to be called, is head of social media at Master & Dynamic, an audio company for the new era. Eric, or "Drummer," as some call him, is a strategist at GLOW Digital Agency.

Drumm thinks brands will never move in the direction of competitive content because of the way marketing is "operationalized." There are just too many stakeholders to allow innovation to happen. Marketing campaigns have too many steps, which makes it seem impossible to do things like this that are outside the box. "Many agencies and brands throw bodies at the work. The more bodies the better is their thinking," said Drumm from Williamsburg, Brooklyn, during a Skype video chat with Carlson and me.

But as you and I know . . . we have worked at agencies where one person did the work of twenty-five people. Many companies like having specialists in silos that can handle the work, but . . . I'd rather go with an agency where there are less people and those people wear many different hats. Whenever you start a campaign where twenty-five people from the brand and agency side need to be in a meeting, you have to check off every box that applies to every part of a department. There really is no reason that [with] a smaller team you can't have all of those things work in harmony.

Carlson noted that some agencies and brands are too rooted in "traditional trajectories" for their eclectic workforce. If they could think outside the box within their marketing roles, she said, they could think outside the box in how they also dish out marketing.

"My entire career has been working in social media, yet there are so many areas within social media where companies can specialize and capitalize on. They only see the role of amplification." She said that her liberal arts background has helped her in areas where those with pure business degrees or marketing majors may have a disadvantage.

I [had] a more traditional liberal arts background. . . . At Hofstra University, I took lots of courses in humanities, art, foreign literature. . . . It forces you to understand the context of different people. The difference I've seen between [me] and other marketers is the ability . . . to tell a story where you can contextualize from different customer scenarios. Too many marketers get mired simply in data and only the data.

Drumm jumped in quickly to note that some companies don't favor 360-degree backgrounds.

There are agencies that don't appreciate a well-rounded background in marketing. They simply hire based on the singular syndrome. They want someone who does creative or analytics. This creates territorial problems. I had a creative tell me at Ogilvy & Mather that I couldn't be a creative director because I wasn't a copywriter, even though I wrote six television commercials.

According to Carlson, that type of traditional, rigid outlook and hiring practice may actually cause some firms to be less competitive.

> The traditional career trajectory for marketing is very linear. I was always given career advice that "you should have this position within three years," then "you should have this position and salary in four years; this one in five years." People excel based on earned experience in an area. What's happened in our economy is you've required people to dip into so many new skills because they are forced to learn them. You have to know how to communicate with people. When I was working at Sprinklr, they valued analytics and were data heavy. They hired me because I was the opposite of that. I was the only person that could talk to people and clients. You'd have one guy that would try to explain numbers and the customers wouldn't get it and then I would use analogies beyond the math and they would understand. The way the economy is you have two people doing five different jobs each. Much of this forces the smarter marketers to become more ambitious and learn elements on the job.

Carlson thinks that even good storytellers may have an expiration date in marketing.

> For things you come across that are of higher value, good companies can't just have stories, or storytellers. They need to have missions. The CEO of one company involved in air travel decided he wanted to be the most sustainable and the greenest company in the world. Focusing on this allows companies to focus on their mission to make the whole world better. Good marketing goes back to a good company, good culture, and good leaders.

This swing away from stories to missions is probably why conventional marketing may finally be peaking. Frank Rose agreed this is the beginning of the end of conventional marketing. He based this on a number of signals.

Story worlds can't be hermetic. They need to be porous enough for people to pass in and out of them at will. But the most fundamental requirement for immersion may be the hardest to achieve: the conspiratorial whisper. The time when brand marketers could dictate what people see, hear, and think is long past, if it ever existed at all. Now they invite people into their world and hope enough will stay to make the effort worthwhile.

CASE-IN-POINT
Swipe Right for Ava

I didn't get to attend SXSWi, Austin's legendary interactive media festival, in 2015, but I followed the action on Twitter. It was a noisy week with startups and brands trying to stay above the fray, but then I noticed something in my feed that fit the mold of this "conspiratorial whisper" noted by both Rose and Boyd.

A twenty-five-year-old named Ava was interacting with users on Twitter telling them to log into Tinder, a real-time dating chat app. What many of the attendees didn't at first know during Ava's aggressive courting of them (obviously her handlers programmed her to engage with males using #SXSWi hashtags on Twitter or Tinder) was that same week *Ex Machina*, the film featuring her character, was debuting at the 2015 SXSW film festival.

While many thought they were making small talk with a potential connection, they realized the truth when Ava sent them to her Instagram page showcasing photos and videos of the film. While psychologically it probably bummed out many young men who thought they were going to hook up with Ava, it attracted their attention in a very noncorporate manner, allowing them to be part of the "enchanted state."

In fact, almost all cases of the best disruptive marketing usually involve zero product marketing or real advertising. The key to disruptive marketing compared to conventional marketing is that it's not about selling anything; it is about becoming immersed in an ongoing conversation.

[handwritten marginal note: Create not advertise that you never want to end convo in college]

[handwritten note at bottom: From Selling   To Immersive Convo]

When did this new norm begin? Well, since language is the original social medium, disruptive models are likely to have existed as far back as ancient Egypt, when citizens bartered for goods and services. The first modern-day formation of disruptive marketing began to take root in the late 1990s.

CHAPTER 2
THE DISRUPTIVE CONTINUUM
Perpetual Change

AFTER WEAF'S DISRUPTIVE experiment to make radio profitable, that business model took over media until Yahoo! emerged in 1994, making it evident that a handful of media sources would no longer be feeding people information. Instead, people could search for things based on intent and find an abundance of possibilities, solutions, and answers.

FROM SPACE AND TIME TO USER INTENT
TO INTERACTION AND IMMERSION

While the behavior of search engines is indeed different from what mass media have to offer, the advertising models on Yahoo! were still based on the same old premise of space and time, with advertisers bidding for space in special ads appearing above the "organic" results of keyword searches.

Fast-forward to 2007: we were no longer chained to a clunky laptop. Searches went mobile with the advent of the iPhone and iOS operating system. While not the first smartphone on the scene, the iPhone disrupted the marketing landscape by allowing developers to create experiences, solutions, and services for interested customers who used the phone as their primary communications tool. Soon it wasn't only about searching for information on a mobile device but also about connecting with others on Facebook, Twitter, and LinkedIn. When brands saw this, they began to realize they didn't have to buy space and time; they could begin to target their messages based on audience data or user intent modeling.

In the course of a hundred years, the world evolved from one of space and time to one of audience and intent. Over the next five years, it will tip toward interaction and immersion, along with customer-designed and customer-created products and the Internet of Things (IoT), the global network of connected physical items such as electronics, software, and sensors. Technology has changed and will continue to change how we evolve in the next hundred years as a result of its effect on human behavior.

While immersion is hardly the last stop on this train, it is the next one that disruptive marketers will have to tackle. And it looks like nothing they've experienced in the past ten years. Disruptive marketers are trying to figure out this new landscape in the most organic way possible from a user experience perspective, while conventional marketers continue to pound us with messages we long ago abandoned.

Because the new normal is filled with uncertainty, it requires the disruptive marketing mindset to be constantly curious rather than to settle for the data it has. And Tinder's "Ava" campaign is a perfect blueprint. Most likely it was seen neither as a success nor as a failure, but simply as a way to inform future promotions and engagement for the film industry. Conventional marketing mindsets have start-and-stop periods in which the campaign runs from one set date to another. But the digital world has no off switch. At any given moment, somewhere in the world, someone is interested in an immersive state.

Disruptive marketers never rest on their laurels. Data is being generated all the time. So how does one use it to gain a competitive advantage?

Data and Disruption: The Competitive Edge

In the early 1990s, the main player in search engines was Yahoo!. Yet, as of this writing, it controls only about 13 percent of search results in the United States. What happened?

Yahoo! search had no real algorithm with which to assess the importance of the results served up on the search engine results page (SERP), the page you get when you search using keywords, phrases, or latent natural language such as, "Where is the nearest pizza shop in Park Slope, Brooklyn?"

In a garage in Menlo Park, California, a small company called Google looked at this, and early on began to seek search results that weren't simply efficient but also disruptive to how Yahoo! and others operated in the space. Using data formulated into an algorithm, Google figured out that users sought a ranking of what was important on the web. This ranking was dubbed "PageRank" (after its creator, Larry Page). PageRank works by counting the number and quality of links to a page to get a rough estimate of how important the website is. The underlying assumption is that the more important a website is, the likelier it is to receive more links from other websites. It's not the only algorithm Google uses to order search-engine results, but it was Google's first, and its best known.

Yahoo! had way more resources and staff, but they weren't thinking about customer experience or user interfaces and design. They simply ran things based on what they thought worked best based on a conventional mindset.

When you think about what will work for your marketing as a business, but you don't consider the customer or user experience based on the design of your products, services, solutions, design, or messages, you're simply not going to last long in this new immersive era. Before the information age, it was much more difficult for customers to get information about anything. Information was scarce, and most companies liked it that way. Today that paradigm is inverted. In fact, it is more difficult for companies to hide what customers say—the good or the bad—about their products or services.

In the conventional marketing model, messages are disseminated using a top-down approach by one ownership team (usually a marketer or marketing department) from company to customer.

In disruptive marketing, communications and conversations are disseminated bottom up, top down, side to side, and back to front by many individuals, including people who don't even work for the company. Sometimes these messages are 100 percent user generated—neither made nor even disseminated by the brand. Owing to the social web, customer-made messages are likely to spread faster than a brand-to-customer approach, thanks to application programming interfaces (APIs).

While many conventional marketers write about the era of digital transformation with blog posts about content, mobile technology, and social media, we will delve into the more important part of how to stay competitive in a world of constant change by focusing on what is key in disruptive marketing. I dub this "The Joy of Next," a phrase used by psychologist Daniel Gilbert in his book *Stumbling on Happiness*.

DISRUPTIVE MARKETING:
IMAGINE THE FUTURE, THEN MAKE IT HAPPEN

The personality trait of a disruptive marketer is centered on what, according to Daniel Gilbert, is believed to be the brain's greatest achievement: "its ability to imagine episodes that do not exist in the realm of the real, and it is this ability that allows us to think about the future."

The ability to imagine a future state is the human brain's most important attribute. And it's the thing we need to use more of—ignoring the obvious and conventional—in the world today.

Google's Eric Schmidt and Jonathan Rosenberg noted one way they ascribe to this "future state" forward-thinking philosophy: people who work at Google don't fit into silos anymore. That would be too conventional in terms of the twenty-first-century definition of a knowledge worker. According to their book *How Google Works*,

> [Google employees] are multidimensional, usually combining technical depth with business savvy and creative flair. In other words, they are not knowledge workers, at least not in the traditional sense. They are a new kind of animal, a type we call a "smart creative," and they are the key to achieving success in the Internet Century.

CASE IN POINT
Software at Scale

In 2006, when I was working in the startup world, businesses understood the power of mobile phones, but no one was thinking about how they would be the main conduit for communication in the next decade. The cost of running an operation consisting of marketing clouds, analytical measurement dashboards, programmatic buying modules, social listening tools, APIs, and video-editing suites enabling marketing in real time was non existent. Marketing departments required lots of people at scale to operate.

Today, however, depending on the type of business, departments that once involved hundreds of workers can now be run by five people, or possibly even one person. While analytics have helped reshape marketing, they also have reshaped how we communicate and create.

In his influential 1937 article "The Nature of the Firm," economist Ronald Coase identified high transaction costs as the reason companies had grown so large. Companies did almost all their work internally because it was too costly to contract out services, supplies, and vending. Today, however, marketing costs have decreased because of the tools available to operate a business. In fact, you may be familiar with this image of the marketing tech landscape: there are so many companies to help with marketing that chiefmartec.com has been producing an infographic annually noting what the marketing technology landscape looks like.

In 2015, there were approximately 1,876 companies representing 43 different marketing technology categories like data visualization, mobile analytics, and collaboration tools, to name a few.

The world is littered with companies (many of which employ only a few people)—ranging from sole proprietorships to Fortune 500s—looking to empower the marketing initiatives of other companies. So, what is the new normal? It's figuring out the best tools for your business—based on its objectives and operations—to take advantage of this new landscape and differentiate your product by using empathy.

Geoffrey Colon
@djgeoffe

Disruptive marketing and growth hacking will ultimately replace conventional marketing. #disruptivefm

3:34 AM — 29 Feb 2016

How do we deploy these tools? To answer this question, let's return to Rebecca "Reb" Carlson, who enjoys analyzing how companies strategically align their resources to make an impact.

Enchanted States of Experience

Rebecca Carlson thinks that most brands are still using the conventional approach to marketing, whereby companies develop products and services and then "go to market" with them, hoping that their communication strategies will attract new customers—and in some cases, retain customers. She says,

> I've been thinking a lot about . . . how data (especially social listening, which I have firsthand experience with) is leveraged—or *not* leveraged—by marketers. The most disruptive tech out there seems to be done by developers, not brands. Social media and content in my opinion are the most effective ways for brands to personally connect with consumers, but Nike I think is making strides in connecting through data provided by consumers [Nike's running and training apps, along with their Fuel Band]. An example where data has been intrusive is that classic story about the guy who found out his daughter was pregnant based on the coupons Target sent.

Carlson is skeptical about where the majority of marketing now stands. She adds,

I don't think many brands are currently leveraging data in disruptive ways. I think there is a bigger interest in quantifying the efforts made through content marketing and visual communication. Image recognition technology is definitely a big focus within social listening platforms; currently engines don't pick up when someone posts a photo of a Coca-Cola can [and] doesn't tag it. Being able to collect that data would be invaluable, especially now that communication has become so visual (GIFs, emojis, Snapchats, etc.). *SOCIAL LISTENING ⇒ SOCIAL RECOGNITION*

With the advent of personal communications technology (the smartphone), the coming world of connected devices and applications (Internet of Things), and the ability for companies to crowdsource new product ideas, the conventional marketing model is becoming more and more irrelevant. So how does one pivot to relevancy?

CASE IN POINT
Trend Laboratories

The best way into disruptive marketing is not necessarily to tap into more marketing, messaging, advertising, or technology but, rather, to tap into the Zeitgeist of your customers' emotions. This is easier said than done, because it requires being more human in your approach, less formulaic, and less governed "by the rules."

Instead of following established rules, disruptive marketers must be aware of what's on the horizon. For this reason, we need to study emerging trends. They are the best indicators of people's behavior—and never forget, it's people who create and drive what's in front of us.

When I was at a small independent agency named Bond Strategy and Influence (formerly called Electric Artists), the CEO and founder, Marc Schiller, held monthly "Trend Labs" at which he compiled a list of trends he sent quarterly to clients, and those clients welcomed the information because it gave them a competitive and differentiating advantage in the marketplace.

Following Marc's example, here is a Trend Labs knockoff that you can use as you think about the world of disruptive marketing.

TEN TRENDS ALL MARKETERS SHOULD CONSIDER

1. **Mobile will be the dominant platform.** Intelligent devices— smartphones, tablets, watches, wearable gadgets, glasses, microchips, HoloLens, and others—will reshape and remix the marketing world. As we shift to a world of intelligent devices, marketing will strike up an even more personalized relationship with customers. Those who can do it faster than their competition will lead in this evolving category.

2. **Transparency will be part of all successful business-customer relationships.** Customers want more engagement from companies. Companies locked into a conventional broadcast model are failing. By 2020, customers will have an even greater expectation of transparency. Authentic companies, including those that admit their mistakes (a trend called "flawsome"), will be heavily rewarded, as will companies that make social responsibility a main part of their culture. Such actions help them form a connection with their customers.

3. **Content is the new currency.** In May 2013, I wrote a *Fast Company* article, "Is Content the New Currency?" explaining that content, especially educational and entertainment content, is a key part of people's lives that will not change in the foreseeable future. However, because content isn't static, new forms such as virtual reality, video games, 3D, and 4D are being issued on platforms that include Oculus Rift and Xbox. Soon, the wearable HoloLens will reshape how content is made. This is one area where disruptive marketing can set a new standard for engaging content.

4. **User-generated content will be the most disruptive.** The power of user-generated content will surpass that of branded content, as brands begin to relinquish control of their own marketing to customers. From online reviews to social media posts and blogs, this means there will be a strong need for brands to create a positive impact in their consumers' minds. In response to this model of user-generated content production, content co-creation between brands and consumers will become a popular trend.

5. **Social networks will become an ecosystem to rival the original Internet.** Social networks have the full potential to

become not just one of the channels but *the* channel—possibly another Internet in and of itself. We're already seeing what we call social, interest, and economic "graphs"—places where people are connected based on a unique commonality. These graphs are growing by leaps and bounds owing to mobile, broadband, and high-quality content on platforms like Facebook, Instagram, Twitter, Tumblr, LinkedIn, Pinterest, and Snapchat.

6. **Brands will act as their own multimedia, bypassing press and publishers.** By cultivating a brand community and culture with their customers, brands will begin to collaborate with their audiences (as opposed to simply trying to sell to them), creating loyalists and brand advocates. In the future, the seeds of branding and marketing efforts will be rooted in what customers are talking about and making. Customer responses and feelings toward the brand will dictate future product development or enhancement. If the customers are happy, they'll gladly wear the marketer's hat and do what is needed to bring the brand to others in their interest or social graphs.

7. **Brands that focus on Generation Z will have the advantage.** The post-Millennial generation will be even more demanding than its predecessors, and brands will need to acknowledge that. For legacy companies, simply updating older marketing that targeted Millennials won't be enough. By 2023 there will be a shift. Companies created by Millennials—such as Facebook, Instagram, or Snapchat—may have to pivot their entire product and strategy to survive. Generation Z will demand that companies be in business for something other than pure profit. Capitalism is about to be reshaped, and those who think solely about revenue as a sign of success will be sorely mistaken and rightfully abandoned.

8. **Most disruptive marketing will be around products, not service.** While service companies aim to create happy customers and look forward to contract renewals or positive social sentiments, product companies thrive on innovation and the future state. What exists in the here and now may be good, but what will exist in the future can and should be vastly improved. So, for marketers of the future, customer

satisfaction and retention will not be enough. Innovative products and solutions will create more value for customers.

9. **Personalized, data-driven disruptive marketing will become the norm.** There is a difference between data-driven disruptive marketing and interruptive marketing. While the former is relationship oriented, whereby content acts as a currency to build trust, the latter is nothing but old-school push messaging in a shiny new digital wrapper. Marketers who focus on building relationships around good products will be rewarded, while fake fast followers with shabby products and poor service will be ostracized.

10. **Tracking metrics will be more accurate.** Today most businesses measure marketing success by looking at hollow "vanity" metrics such as impressions, likes, shares, or engagement rates. We're still developing sophisticated means to mine the right data. The future will witness the rise of better analytical tools to help marketers gauge success in terms of emotional and cultural relevance, as well as ROI.

QUOTE

Often it is technology companies that employ disruptive marketing strategies. Computers, phones, apps, and electronic devices or services can be shipped as a minimally viable product, and then be updated regularly while in the possession of their customers. Think of every app you have ever downloaded. What versions are they now on?

As the world shifts to the point where a brick-and-mortar store that sells children's clothes, or even your local pizza shop, must operate like a technology company, the techniques of disruptive marketing become applicable to every business. (Think I'm kidding? Zeek's, a local pizza shop in Seattle, has one of the better mobile apps for ordering, delivery, and payment. It also keeps your last order on record so you don't have to repeat it if, like me, you eat pretty much the same thing every Friday night.)

Four Goals for Disruptive Marketers

So, what goals and objectives should you adopt as you take on disruptive marketing or look to strengthen it within your organization?

Here are four that I believe should always be the true north of disruptive marketers:

1. **Designing products, services, solutions, or causes that meet the demands of an emerging market.** It's no longer enough just to market products, especially products nobody wants in the first place. Marketers must help in the actual design and user experience, based on their understanding of people's emotions. This spills into . . .

2. **Reshaping or reengineering an existing product, service, solution, or cause so that it meets the demands of customers unsatisfied by current offerings.** Many companies give up on customers who don't like their products. But that attitude could stunt your sustained growth and put you out of business. Sometimes this means blowing up your old products (PowerPoint) for new ones (Sway) that fit the new norm. You do this via . . .

3. **Customer-centricity.** Every move you make needs to be from the point of view of the customer, even if it might not benefit the company's bottom line. This is where the art of immersion or enchantment fits in. Customers want to go deep into your world, not simply be told about it. The best way to understand that customer is through . . .

4. **Emotional intelligence.** The most disruptive marketers combine the concept of design thinking with a radical way of operating—that is, they don't think of their business simply as a cohort of employees and their target market as a segment of customers. Disruptive marketing blurs that line to the point where customers and employees are one and the same, and they use communication tools to create products in tandem.

That last point is forward thinking. I can't name one company that has reached that state of nirvana yet. But if we pay more attention to human behavior, design, and psychology than to technology, this is ultimately what customers want and crave, and what disruptive marketing can deliver. A movement like this will ultimately produce some of the most innovative solutions the world has seen. But how do you make that happen?

Through emerging communications. Disruptive marketing won't work if the entire company isn't along for the journey. You can't just have a few people in the marketing department trying to do this. According to a 2014 Gartner report, "Digital business success will require organizations to take bold actions, including inventing new business models and changing the way they function. Gartner predicts that by 2017, 70 percent of successful business models will rely on deliberately unstable processes designed to shift with *customers' needs.*"

Resistance to this new way of thinking and acting can be costly. Eighty-nine percent of the companies that were in the Fortune 500 sixty years ago are now gone. That is the force of creative destruction, or apathy about doing things differently, or thinking punk rock about how to shake things up.

Ray Wang, author of *Disrupting Digital Business*, uses scarier terminology to describe what may happen to companies that don't adopt disruptive marketing: "Since 2000, 52 percent of the names on the Fortune 500 list are gone, either as a result of mergers, acquisitions or bankruptcies. The changes are the result of digital business models creating disruption in the marketplace." While about 5 percent of organizations are leaders in proactively transforming their business models to adapt to the latest technologies (Microsoft, Oracle, Apple, Amazon, Facebook, and Uber among them), Wang says about 30 percent of companies are laggards who don't want to change their business models. "Digital Darwinism is unkind to those who wait. Anybody, even the smallest startup can overtake a large Fortune 500 company because it's the non-traditional competitors that are creating new customers and new customer classes." Wang adds that while the average age of a company on the S&P 500 was sixty years old in 1960, it will continue to shrink and be twelve years old by 2020, a compression of five times.

While all of this may appear scary and fill some people with unease, it should make you feel excited. With a new normal comes the potential for new opportunities.

CHAPTER 3

CREATIVE DISRUPTION IN
THE ANTI ORGANIZATION AGE

A creative economy is the fuel of magnificence.

—RALPH WALDO EMERSON

"HEY, SO YOU want to find an apartment together?"

I was speaking into the old gray telephone handset with big orange buttons that hung from my parents' kitchen wall in Bethlehem, Pennsylvania. On the other end of the line was my friend Eric "DJ Strobe" Cohen, talking from his apartment on Second Avenue in New York City's East Village.

"Uh, yeah, but we have to make sure we have an extra room for my music studio," said Eric, "because that's a source of additional revenue for me."

"No worries, I'm down for that," I noted. "We also need to make sure we have a spot for the turntables."

Eric enthusiastically replied, "Oh yeah!"

CASE IN POINT
Growth Hacking in Hell's Creative Kitchen

It was May of 1996. After bumming around for two years postcollege, trying to figure out the meaning of life (translation: waiting tables, ↓

DJing at a nightclub, doing freelance design work for small businesses, and basically trying to survive while living with my parents), a close colleague offered me a job doing international marketing for what seemed to me to be every unknown musician on the planet. It wasn't a glamorous job, but it got my foot in the door. The industry was no stranger to me. I'd spent much of my time since 1991 as a radio and club disc jockey, and I'd been networking with a few in the industry on early Internet chat boards and via email.

So, when the call came with the salary offer ($350 a week, no benefits), all I needed to do was find an affordable place to live. Enter my buddy Eric.

The place we eventually found was in Hell's Kitchen, at the time a pretty rough Manhattan neighborhood with a dark history. Inhabited by poor and working-class Irish Americans at the turn of the nineteenth century, it had been known for its Irish gangs and, even in the 1970s, as a place where both the Irish and Italian American mafias carried out hits.

Hell's Kitchen at the time was nothing like it is today. On the night we moved in, we couldn't leave our apartment because the police were carrying out a drug raid right outside. To us—two twenty-something members of the creative class—this was the perfect location to begin our future-of-work experiment.

Although Eric worked at a computer store by day, his real craft was as a music producer and DJ. In 2016, this fact barely registers—everyone under thirty is now a DJ/producer—but in 1996, the barrier to entry was formidable, especially when compared to today's easy access via software and social networks.

Eric had a small one-room studio (literally our living room in the loft space we called home) in which he would produce, remix, and master recordings. There was no need for a high-end studio with lots of fancy equipment, since software and a few pieces of hardware were his main tools along with a good mixing desk, some audio plug-ins, a laptop computer, and high-end headphones.

In 1997, a major record label asked Eric if he would remix a song for one of its young singer-songwriters, Jennifer Paige. The label wanted different versions to give it more of a chance of being played on radio. Eric obliged and asked the label to send him the "stem" of the singer's vocals. (A stem is a mixed group of audio sources.) Later, Eric and I had a good laugh over the fact that the label representative was clueless about what Eric wanted.

Eric didn't need to meet the artist. He didn't need her to re-record any vocals in the studio. All he needed was the original vocals so that he could produce an entirely new soundscape. Eric requested delivery via bike messenger of the vocal stem on digital audiotape so he could dump it into his software and build a whole new musical arrangement around the vocals.

Nowadays, a stem is not a big deal; artists regularly put stems up on YouTube so that any producer can download and remix their songs. Back then, in that Hell's Kitchen apartment, we were almost twenty years ahead of the curve. Today, songs are remixed to piggyback off another more popular artist's name. (As Pablo Picasso said, "Good artists copy but great artists steal.") This is the essence of "growth hacking." At the intersection of marketing and engineering, growth hacking is now being used by many startups to gain audience share.

In the late 1990s we were on the fringe of what has become the creative participatory (gig) economy that drives the world economy. No brands created this. In fact, corporations that try to enter it usually meet with distrust. A true community supports this world organically, and no brand can ever control it.

BRANDS AND CREATIVITY
IN THE ANTI ORGANIZATION AGE

Do brands foster creativity? It's doubtful. Despite all the articles online about how to foster a culture of creativity at brands, companies peddling products are the last place people turn for creative expression. On the other hand, brands could learn a lot from the outsider art.

Art has always been about what one feels and what one wants to express. It's also about making a personal statement. Art contributes to the world around us when it makes people feel something as a result of their interaction with it. For decades, brands wanted their

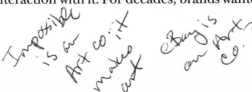

statement and narrative to be the only story that customers heard. For this reason, brands were at the forefront of de-emphasizing art. As far as they were concerned, it was unimportant to the sales process. In the early 1990s, with the rise of personal computing and software such as PowerPoint, organizations concentrated solely on value process, asking, "How do we sell us?" "How do we talk about us?" Most ad and marketing campaigns at that time were brand centered. The only art was found in slogans, like one from Pepsi that showed pop art versions of their cans and the tagline: "Our idea of pop art. New Cool Cans."

That was in a read-only world. Yet despite the changes, many brands still don't seem to understand that we now live in a read/write/remix world, and such narratives leave little space for creative expression or third-party partnerships. However, in 2013, art came roaring back into many marketing campaigns, including those for W Hotels, Lincoln cars, Ketel One Vodka, and Samsung Electronics. You could say that many on Madison Avenue were adopting the slogan *Ars gratia artis*, or "Art for art's sake," in order to speak the same language as a young generation that appreciated art as a common language.

Today, with platforms like Instagram, Snapwire, and Olapic ushering in creativity for any smartphone user, brands are beginning to backtrack and position themselves again in the middle of modern design and technology. After all, these actions now help generate revenue. For many brands, creative directors, and media, the appeal of using "social photography" for commercial purposes is growing. First, the variety of potential photos is nearly infinite, the visuals often have a personality or authenticity that traditional stock photos lack, and there's plenty of opportunity for valuable engagement with fans and customers. Second, any mobile camera user can now be a photographer on behalf of the brand.

That said, does anyone really want to create brand art? For much of human history, economics de-emphasized making, creating, innovating, and producing art because it didn't create capital. However, now that brands are moving away from capital as their main reason to exist, they are beginning to understand that creative imagery is a key piece in connecting with people. Could disruptive marketing help brands gain an advantage?

THE MOVE TOWARD THE CREATIVE ECONOMY

To better understand how we came to live in today's creative economy, we need to understand the history and evolution of the economy at large.

The two driving principles of the industrial age were control and certainty. For businesses to control individual decision makers and create processes that could be repeated over and over for success, the idea of the corporation emerged. In what is considered by many to be the most influential management book ever written, 1956's *The Organization Man*, William H. Whyte described the expansion of the corporate business model and explained why, in the post–World War II era, when Americans had shed the idea of rugged individualism in work, management and marketing organizations and groups could make better decisions than the individual.

With this in mind, it made the most sense from a career standpoint to serve the organization rather than one's own creative passions and desires. The corporation acted as a shell to help businesses, which were inherently risk averse, manage in uncertain times. Whyte ripped heavily on the idea of risk averseness, noting that it creates workers who face zero consequences as long as they make no mistakes.

The scenario Whyte documented seems a far cry from how business operates now. Or is it? For some brands, you wouldn't think they ever left the twentieth century—or 1956, for that matter.

For much of the twentieth century, the conventional wisdom was that the only thing required for success in business was to synchronize systems. This idea is rooted in the left-brain thinking of the knowledge economy, a concept that cropped up as early as the 1960s. However, as W. Brian Arthur noted in *Complexity and the Economy*, "The world is to a large extent organic and algorithmic." This is one reason super platforms that share vast amounts of information are more powerful than static websites. Having elements of organic sharing and algorithmic filtering in business is like the air and water necessary for life. Consequently, influence and reputation are the new currency. Brands are now tasked with creating objectives that capture the imagination of a new generation of customers.

The driving design principles of today's transformative age are empowerment and opportunity exploitation. Structural change has become mandatory as a result of shifting behavioral and economic changes. There are just a few problems holding many companies back from this transformation. One is that they have failed to understand that, in the age of what many of us dub "cognitive capitalism," the new economic system may not place as much emphasis on revenue as it does on persuasion and influence.

MARKETING IN THE AGE OF ABUNDANCE

In their sprint to force demand for their products, conventional marketers seem to forget one thing about this new reality: information is abundant. Even physical goods and intellectual property are free. Paul Mason, journalist for the *Guardian*, explains it this way:

> We're surrounded not just by intelligent machines but by a new layer of reality centered on information. Consider an airliner: a computer flies it; it has been designed, stress-tested and "virtually manufactured" millions of times; it is firing back real-time information to its manufacturers. On board are people squinting at screens connected, in some lucky countries, to the internet. Seen from the ground it is the same white metal bird as in the James Bond era. But it is now both an intelligent machine and a node on a network. It has information content and is adding "information value" as well as physical value to the world. On a packed business flight, when everyone's peering at Excel or PowerPoint, the passenger cabin is best understood as an information factory. But what is all this information worth? You won't find an answer in the accounts: intellectual property is valued in modern accounting standards by guesswork. A study for the SAS Institute in 2013 found that, in order to put a value on data, neither the cost of gathering it, nor the market value or the future income from it could be adequately calculated. Only through a form of accounting that included non-economic benefits, and risks, could companies actually explain to their shareholders what their data was really worth. Something is broken in the logic we use to value the most important thing in the modern world.

In other words, since the advent of the web in the early 1990s, and the social web in the early 2000s, as well as the Internet of Things, which will arrive in the next ten to fifteen years, economics has been centered on a condition of scarcity. Yet the most dynamic force facing the modern world is an abundance of information and solutions. This is a curse to brands that think they have the only product worthy of a customer's attention. And it's a curse to brands that still believe they need only a handful of channels to promote their products, solutions, and messages.

In 1960, there were only five marketing channels, but as of this writing, there are more than seventy. If we apply Moore's Law to marketing channels, this number will double or triple every two years.

The Impact of Loss of Control over Marketing Channels

The other underlying issue—the bigger one, in fact—is that corporations are not structured to endure these ongoing changes, especially in marketing. Brands have little control over these marketing channels because users will interact with one another before they will interact with a company. The corporation along with the conventional marketing mindset is designed to avoid radical shifts and to incrementally deal with these scenarios. Their DNA is not built on a double helix structure that contains the elements of transformation and reimagination found in startups.

As a result, the majority of corporations miss out on the opportunities that exist in the creative economy. They wouldn't even know how to find an Eric in his Hell's Kitchen apartment or how to program a music channel for their brand on Spotify, or how to engage in any cultural marketing because—to conventional thinkers—activities like this don't drive revenue.

If corporate brands were the only players in our global economy, I would tell them not to sweat it. But the economy isn't made up solely of multinational corporations. Small and startup businesses, which drive the most economic growth, are ever more capable of taking advantage of the creative economy. Their DNA isn't wired like a large company's. They may have issues of their own—scarcity of financial resources, for example—but that can be an advantage in a world filled with an increasing number of "freemium" growth empowerment options, software to scale, and attention-grabbing nurture streams.

Geoffrey Colon
@djgeoffe

Corporations are risk averse. This is a disadvantage in the creative economy. #disruptivefm

6:32 PM—21 Feb 2016

We know that the brands of the future will look a lot different from the brands of today. However, many brands are taking a long time to figure out exactly what they will look like. And all the while, the clocks are ticking and the business models are being burned to the ground. We know that over the next twenty years, machine intelligence will play a much larger role in value creation. Mobile devices and the Internet of Things will change how we engage with others.

It is only by algorithmically programming all the routine processes that organizations will be able to free up the creative space for differentiated and innovative offerings. The time previously spent "managing machines" and pouring resources into operations will be repurposed into creative output. This is one reason companies that put more emphasis on free time to explore ideation and innovation have an added advantage in the new economy. Reshaping the economy from one based on knowledge to one based on creativity also involves reshaping the way marketing will work.

In 2014, I created a spreadsheet to document the amount of time I spent on three areas of my business: creative, operations, and management. The first area covered any creative input or output to drive my business. The second dealt with time sheets, invoices, purchase orders, and so on. The third dealt with managing my team. Here's what that chart looked like, based on forty-seven sixty-hour workweeks:

TOTAL HOURS WORKED = 2,820

- Creative = 282, or 10 percent
- Operations = 1,692, or 60 percent
- Management = 846, or 30 percent

I put the most time into the operational side of the business and the least into creative. Wouldn't it make more sense if my time as a marketer—mainly a creative and artistic field intermixed with data—took up 60 percent of my time and the operational took up 10 percent? Shouldn't the time spent on these two areas be flipped? Big companies are at a major disadvantage when they compete in the creative economy when they have scenarios like this!

In 2014, I had the privilege of taking part in the Kellogg School of Management certification program at Northwestern University. It was a wonderful experience. Professors broke down some of the things that all organizations must contend with in moving forward. The media are no longer in the hands of the few but, rather, are distributed among the many. As a result, how we use media—and especially imagery—has become the new creative activity. In the words of Lawrence Lessig, author of *Remix: Making Art and Commerce Thrive in the Hybrid Economy*, "Knowledge and manipulation of multi-media technologies is the current generation's form of 'literacy.'"

Guy Debord, author and Marxist critical theorist, foreshadowed this in his 1967 critique, *The Society of the Spectacle*, in which he wrote that images had supplanted genuine human interaction. "All that was once directly lived has become mere representation." We can see much of this in how we interact on platforms such as Facebook and Instagram.

WHAT "UNICORNS" KNOW ABOUT THE CREATIVE ECONOMY

Conventional marketers and brands use these social media platforms as they were built to function. Disruptive marketing takes it a step further and asks, "If the economy is being reshaped to focus on *living* rather than on *having*, what image should we use to convey this enchanted state?" That is, if in a consumer society social life is not about living, but about having, in an immersive creative society, social life is about individuals *making* and *producing*, and receiving commentary and feedback from the crowd by using a variety of communication platforms.

Geoffrey Colon
@djgeoffe

The creative economy is about making things and experiences, not simply consuming and having things. #disruptivefm

6:33 PM—21 Feb 2016

This leads us to a whole new era in the history of civilization. There is no past knowledge from which to draw as we plot the future. This is a difficult problem for the corporate branding model, which uses past data to shape its next moves. Conversely, it gives an advantage to those with creative thinking skills, especially disruptive marketers, especially those with the imagination to paint on a blank digital canvas that correlates with the daily business plan motto: Don't *plan* more, *do* more.

At the same time as we are transforming from an analog to a digital world, we are also accelerating from a knowledge economy to a creative participatory economy. In knowledge-based economies, people are paid to think of linear left-brain answers to complex scenarios. Engineers analyze data and come up with a process, equation, or product. However, because of the massive growth of the web—and specifically search engines like Bing—we rely less on knowledge transfer because everything we need to know can be found with the swipe of our finger on any connected device. Only the most complex issues remain unsolved, and in the next fifty years many of those may well be solved as well.

As a result, the knowledge economy is ceding to a more powerful yet even more complex cognitive, creative economy. John Howkins describes the nature of this economy in his book *The Creative Economy:*

The creative economy consists of the transaction in . . . creative products. Each transaction may have two complementary values, the value of the intangible, intellectual property and the value of the physical carrier or platform (if any). In some industries, such as digital software, the intellectual property value is higher. In others, such as art, the unit cost of the physical object is higher.

If you consider what Howkins is saying, and then look at the stock market and analyze why companies like Facebook, Microsoft, Google, and Apple are so highly valued, you will soon realize it's because their business models have crossed the chasm into this new era. The same can be said about several billion-dollar valuated startups (dubbed "Unicorns," in Silicon Valley tech slang) that understand and have implemented this premise.

Disruptive Marketing in the Creative Economy

It's important to understand how this balance of power is shifting if you are to embrace disruptive marketing in the creative economy. If you sell based on product features, the product gets lost in a field of lookalikes, knockoffs, and re-engineered goods, whereas brands positioned as services—as opposed to products—will stand out from the crowd.

People are looking for experiences, emotions, and feelings, not products, features, or price points. And the web acts as a feedback loop where everyone can find data they can apply to their decision-making process.

Consider how politics is being reshaped in this creative economy. Why aren't middle-of-the-road ideologies good enough for citizens anymore? Is it possible that radical ideas from both the left and right edges of the political spectrum are seeping into the consciousness of the general population because incremental change is no longer fast enough? Is this a global trend? Are people worldwide yearning for the fringe? It seems people won't settle for the way things have always been done. Especially from bland brands.

Richard Florida, author of *The Rise of the Creative Class*, offers another explanation for why branding is shifting. A large percentage of the world's economy is now made up of the "creative class," a highly educated and mobile workforce that, in the past, had been highly sought by brands and advertisers alike. (The other two classes noted by Florida are the "working class" and the "service class.") In an era in which media had yet to fragment, it was easy to reach this audience via media planning, ad buying, and brand messaging. However, Florida gives good economic reasons for the need to pivot brand marketing in the twenty-first century to meet this customer-centric emerging class. Florida explains:

> [T]he Creative Class is the norm-setting class of our time. But its norms are very different: Individuality, self-expression and openness to difference are favored over the homogeneity, conformity and "fitting in" that defined the organization age. Furthermore, the Creative Class is dominant in terms of wealth and income, with its members earning nearly twice as much on average as members of the other two classes.

The New Creative: How We Use Media

The mass media have always held the power for the conventional brand marketer. But for the disruptive marketer, it's simply something to hack into and use in new and imaginative ways. In his 2006 book, *An Army of Davids: How Markets and Technology Empower Ordinary People to Beat Big Media, Big Government and Other Goliaths,* Glenn Reynolds notes how technological change has allowed people more freedom of action in contrast to the "big" establishment organizations that used to function as gatekeepers. The balance of power is flattening out into a more and more level playing field. As a result, how we use media to reach our customers in an attention-deficit economy becomes more imaginative, depending on how we disruptively engage with it.

In 1990, when I entered Pennsylvania's Lehigh University, the library gave me an email address. I used that address quite a bit to send electronic mail to other students and professors. Yet even more exciting than electronic mail was having access via one portal in the college newspaper (*The Brown and White*) newsroom to the World Wide Web. As early as 1991, I would log in and surf it daily to see what was going on in the world. There weren't many websites at that time. If the information existed, and you could find it (which was easy because there was a finite amount of data), you could find answers. Nevertheless, I still relied on gatekeepers who amplified their voices via print media.

Fast-forward to 1998, when much of the information that was available in the physical world became available online. However, the infrastructure was not yet strong enough to support the potential of this new commerce ecosystem. That is, the world was not as mobile as it is today. However, from the ashes of the dotcom era rose today's web 2.0 and the interconnected social web. Data is plentiful. In fact, Google's Eric Schmidt said in 2010, "Every two days we create as much information as we did from the dawn of civilization up until 2003. That's something like five exabytes of data."

Much of this data is user-generated content (UGC) in the form of photos, videos, graphics, GIFs (graphics interchange format), and memes. As marketers, we compete against it, even beyond our normal business competition. Conventional marketing, with its stale messages about value propositions and its narratives about the company's vision, simply won't cut it anymore; those messages are unlikely to be seen, heard, or, most important, felt in this noisy space.

It's the Creative Economy, Stupid!

In early 1992, James Carville, then presidential campaign adviser for Arkansas governor Bill Clinton, hung a sign on a wall in the Little Rock headquarters. His candidate trailed in the presidential race by 30 percentage points. On that paper were three items:

1. Change vs. more of the same.
2. Don't forget health care.
3. It's the economy, stupid.

What was meant for an internal audience tipped into the external and became a rallying cry. Ten months later, Clinton ousted incumbent George H. W. Bush for the presidency.

Carville gained the attention of a population mired in a poor job market and won their hearts and minds through a slogan. It was a simple message, but one that was easily carried in the pre-social web word-of-mouth era.

If that same message was delivered today, it would barely travel past the end of the block, primarily because it lacks creative and immersive UGC to support it. Slogans and words without customer participation are lost on inattentive minds. Unless those words are attached to people we know and trust, we tune them out, just as we would tune out an annoying radio commercial on WEAF-AM.

If today, Carville gave that slogan to a group of "influentials" who were rabid Clinton supporters and said, "I don't care what you do; here's what we believe," those supporters would turn that message into something far more powerful. The story and outcome would be different because each person interprets messages differently and makes them personal based on his or her belief system. Once the message is personal, people identify with it.

CREATIVE MARKETING LESSONS FROM #FERGUSON

It was August 9, 2014. I remember the date because I had just finished wishing my older brother Brian a happy birthday. It was close to 1 AM Eastern Time. I wanted to know what the weather was going to be like in Seattle the next day, but before I checked, I peered at my phone to see what was trending on Twitter.

In third or fourth spot was #Ferguson.

Curious what #Ferguson was about, I clicked on it. I had read in the news earlier about a policeman having shot a civilian, and now it appeared that citizens were taking to the streets in protest. Without many mainstream news sources telling me what was going on, I simply followed the tweets from regular people who were in Ferguson, Missouri, that night. Some of them were horrifying.

That night I turned to all the mainstream news outlets to see what they were doing or saying about the events. None of the major cable news outlets—CNN, MSNBC, and Fox News—were talking about Ferguson. In fact, it took almost another week for those outlets to note what was going on there. But their narrative was too late; by then, citizens had set the tone for the events.

I felt the official news reporters weren't asking questions in an objective manner.

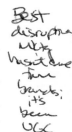

Ferguson, the Black Lives Matter movement, and Occupy Wall Street are good examples of disruptive marketing. Yes, I know what you are saying: "But what are they selling? What is the profit motive?" Earlier I said you must remove both feet from the twentieth century and put them squarely into the twenty-first. Do it now, and you'll see how both disruptive marketing and movements like these are more about collaborative communications than about products or profits.

The Disadvantages of Organizational Models

In the experience economy, anyone can bring attention and meaning to events, messages, and experiences. No longer are these functions the job of a centralized organization. Because disruptive marketers understand this, they design noncentralized hierarchies to help spread the information created by others.

To demonstrate this, let's first take a look at Figure 3-1 which explains organizational models, and then look at decentralized movements like #BlackLivesMatter to see why they are more effective than centralized and controlled brand-marketing campaigns.

The Figure 3-1a model is an organizational hierarchy common to many companies. In a marketing organization, the chief marketing officer (CMO) usually owns the top spot. Below that position are a number of disciplines that control the outputs of siloed groups, such as digital, brand, and social. The hierarchy model doesn't have much intergroup interaction. Nor does it allow for the free flow of information from the bottom up or from other groups or teams within the company. Consequently, many good ideas never see the light of day.

Geoffrey Colon
@djgeoffe

Hierarchies are for the military, not modern businesses or relationship marketing models. #disruptivefm

6:34 PM—21 Feb 2016

Figure 3-1: Conventional Marketing Organization Model
vs. Social Network Model

HIERARCHICAL ORGANIZATION
STRUCTURE

SOCIAL NETWORK

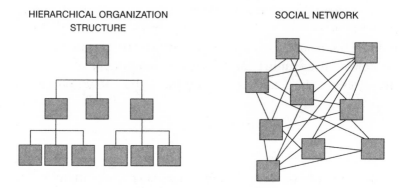

Figure 3-1a: Conventional Marketing Hierarchy

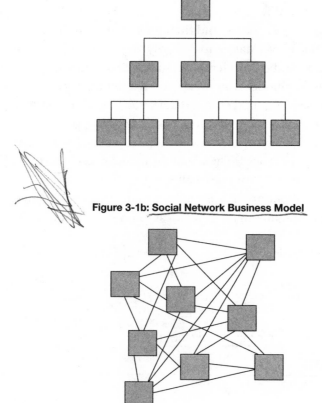

Figure 3-1b: Social Network Business Model

The Figure 3-1b model is a disruptive marketer's playground, on the other hand. In this social network model, anyone and everyone—especially external audiences—owns the messages and can create solutions.

When people ask how organizations can operate without a central leadership figure, what they miss is that central leadership figures (CMOs, in this case) rarely have much, if any, creative power because they spend most of their time on operations and people management. But in a networking model where operations are spread out, good ideas have a better chance of being accepted and adopted quickly and organically.

The Advantages of Decentralized Movements

Black Lives Matter and Occupy Wall Street are often thought of as "decentralized" movements. They don't rely on a leader—and for good reason. Usually, when leaders leave organizations others leave, too. In the case of the social network model (Figure 3-1b), when a top leader leaves the messaging doesn't lose momentum. There are others still generating content and experiences without the need for a "chief" officer to make that happen.

Geoffrey Colon
@djgeoffe

Savvy marketers understand a social business model helps them do more with less. #disruptivefm

6:34 PM—21 Feb 2016

Conventional marketers usually rely on antiquated communication systems like email or even the telephone. The social network model, however, relies more on a business model in which tools like Slack, Yammer, and Jive replace email. Conventional marketers are still relying too much on linear and one-to-one tactics, rather than employing dynamic and many-to-many strategies that help carry messages.

Although it may look as if the sort of instability that a social network model presents will fail, because it lacks a defined and rigid organizational hierarchy, leadership actually plays a bigger role by making sure the organic messages that are created find their way to more people.

STOP HIRING MBAs
Your Business Needs Hybrids to Succeed

AS WE'VE SEEN, the belief that control is part of any marketing efforts today is truly an illusion. The creative economy relies on imagination that derives from day-to-day experience—and this is where MBA strategists are left in the dust. You can't do what you haven't yourself experienced. If you aren't feeling the pulse of your industry, and see how it interacts with other industries, you'll have a hard time moving beyond the conventional.

THE NEW DISRUPTION: INFORMATION JAMMING

Once it is realized that hierarchies are better left to the military, disruptive marketing can spread across a business organization at a rapid rate. We saw this in 2011 with the advent of growth hacking. If we put marketing on fast-forward, we need more than just data-driven measures to move the needle in an attention-starved economy. The new disruption is "information jamming."

The expression is a riff on "radio jamming" and "culture jamming," which are attempts to disrupt establishment processes by using subversive tactics like pirate radio and street art. Information jamming is the term used to describe how disruptive marketers look at the world moving forward. The core belief in information jamming is: *Don't hate the media because they won't help carry your narrative to the desired audience. Do it yourself. Be your own media.*

Information jamming is commonplace among the most radical of disruptive marketers, those who are pushing the envelope into areas—such as measuring the brain's reactions to their messages—that many perceive as unethical or antitrustworthy in terms of customer confidence. David Brooks, my mentor and currently senior vice president of digital and social media strategy at Ogilvy & Mather, wonders if this is the right path for all situations. Regarding the study of customers' neurological reactions to advertising's messaging, he says,

> I have not seen marketing tools that delve into mapping messages and behaviors to things like the amygdala or prefrontal cortex and how they are affected. I think marketing and advertising have always mapped their products to one's feeling better or achieving more in some way. I think what digital technologies will increasingly allow for is "reading" how people are reacting and adjusting what the message is based on the emotional reaction. I expect a debate on this too as it's an area that is clearly controversial.

Because of the controversial, attention-getting nature of this topic, some companies try to own the conversation. Yet this is a lesson the disruptive marketer understands very well. If you find parts of this book controversial, or if you are at odds with some of my predictions or points of view, then I'm doing the very job of disruptive marketer. I'm reaching you in ways that spark emotion and drive conversation.

For decades, brand messaging has tried to evoke "feel good" sentiments. But *debate* is at the heart of information jamming. Indeed, not everyone should agree with brand narratives. Yet, many brands have been reluctant to take a stand, afraid that they'll alienate their customers. But if they don't stand for something, they won't stand for long.

Information jamming means stating a point of view strongly so as to attract attention, spark conversation, and encourage disagreement via content that is not overtly, consciously branded.

CASE IN POINT
Going Viral

The biggest project I have worked on that used information jamming was called "A Boy and His Atom."

In 2012, while I was working for Ogilvy & Mather, David Brooks and I were brought into a meeting. This wasn't unusual. If you work in the agency world, an average day is filled with meetings because they're billable time. But this meeting was different.

We assumed that the creative directors for the IBM account wanted to make another TV ad, which had been the firm's main driver for many years. But we were wrong. They were interested in hearing about how to make content go viral. They, like so many others, had realized that some of the biggest things on the web didn't just happen organically; there were triggers to direct that content to an audience and then have it either spread like a wildfire or die on the vine.

The meeting was interesting. Unlike most meetings, the creative team didn't want a social or digital strategy. They wanted research on the science of sharing. They wanted to know more about what induced people to share content with others. David and I hurried back to our desks, realizing that maybe this big one-hundred-plus-year-old company was finally going to do something different. We just had no clue how different it was going to be.

Earlier that year, the *New York Times* released research on "the psychology of sharing." It was relevant, but to me, too linear an approach to the subject. The writers made it appear that if you identify the six personality types who share content, then you can have successful marketing campaigns. That approach was just too simplistic.

But I did find one nugget of information that others had overlooked. One of the groups identified in the article was dubbed "Hipster." Not really your Williamsburg, Brooklyn, or Capitol Hill (Seattle) hipster, but it certainly was the online hipster who shares cutting-edge content and who works in the creative industries. David and I dug a little deeper. Of those six types of people who share, it wasn't just that hipsters shared cutting-edge content but also that the content was both cutting edge and *unbranded*.

In 2012, the social web was full of branded content, as it is today. Too many brands thought they could stamp their name all over it and people would pay attention. Of course, this is the conventional marketer's arrogance. In all our digging, we couldn't find an example of non-branded company content. Then David stumbled on what we would eventually present to the creative directors as a way to convince IBM not to overtly brand its viral undertaking.

In late August 2011, Chipotle released a film with Willie Nelson covering Coldplay's song "The Scientist." (How come so many innovative things happen in late August? Because many people are on vacation and aren't paying as much attention to their devices, so it's a good time to run tests that go under the popular radar.) "The Scientist" was pure synchronization genius, its content unbranded and inspiring. The only mention of Chipotle was at the end of the film, when it noted "chipotle. com." Otherwise, a viewer would think he or she was watching an animation on sustainable farming.

The song was even available for download on iTunes, with all the proceeds donated to the Chipotle Cultivate Foundation (which they had set up to create a more healthy and sustainable food supply). To date, that video has garnered over nine million views. But views tell only part of the story. Unbranded marketing has swept that organization, including an author series on its in-store cups, entitled "Cultivating Thought," and an original Hulu program called "Farmed and Dangerous." Even more important, Chipotle is a mainstay with Millennial audiences. It has a great product, and its unconventional approach to brand marketing is one of the main reasons why it's been so successful.

Ultimately, IBM agreed and went with content that made the *Guinness Book of World Records* as "The World's Smallest Movie." As of this writing, "A Boy and His Atom" has had 5.6 million views. The movie mentions IBM Research only at the beginning and end; the rest of the 1:33 clip is about data storage. In 2013, the film was awarded several Cannes Lions awards for Best Branded Content.

I find it funny that David and I persuaded the Ogilvy creative directors to come up with unbranded content, and that the result won awards for best branded content! Maybe it's because people actually paid attention to it.

Geoffrey Colon
@djgeoffe

If you want branded content to travel further in the form of shares, unbrand it as much as possible. #disruptivefm

6:35 PM — 21 Feb 2016

eBay quote

If I could go back in time, would I change anything about that project? Yes, I would have used data about the lack of women in tech fields and the difficulty of recruiting women into science and technology positions. And I would have retitled the film "A Girl and Her Atom." Had IBM gone this route, I think the film would have captured the concerns about the scarcity of women in technical fields, and the company would have been seen as a leader in this area.

WHY MFAs ARE STRONGER MARKETERS THAN MBAs

Apple never invested heavily in marketing, preferring to build great products and save money on fixed costs. Then something strange happened: Samsung phones, which feature a different operating system (the open-source and Google-owned Android) and a bigger screen, began to pick up market share in 2013. Soon, as Samsung was seeing major adoption across various markets, Apple moved toward television commercials in an attempt to differentiate its products from the competition. One ad, at the end of 2014, showed the iPhone not simply as a phone but instead as a mobile creative tool featuring a user who was an artist. Shortly after this ad aired, Apple reported that iPhone sales boomed, while Samsung reported flat sales or marginal growth.

Creativity in the new economy isn't simply about selling; it's also about how you can stand out from the pack. How does a brand survive in a world filled with copycats, reverse-engineered products, and free intellectual property and still be relevant? Much of this answer is going to come from a new way of thinking that involves art, science, math, psychology, and media. It doesn't align with the resounding corporate or higher education culture that says MBAs are the best qualified to occupy marketing roles.

Richard Florida explains what the creative economy means from a commodity-meets-people perspective:

> Creativity is multidimensional and comes in many mutually reinforcing forms. It is a mistake to think, as many do, that creativity can be reduced to the creation of new blockbuster inventions, new products and new firms. In today's economy, creativity is pervasive and ongoing: We constantly revise and enhance every product, process and activity imaginable, and fit them together in new ways. Moreover, technological and economic creativity are nurtured by and interact with artistic and cultural creativity. This kind of interplay is evident in the rise of whole new industries from computer graphics to digital music and animation. Creativity also requires a social and economic environment that can nurture its many forms. Max Weber said long ago that the Protestant ethic provided the underlying spirit of thrift, hard work and efficiency that motivated the rise of early capitalism. In similar fashion, the shared commitment to the creative spirit in its many, varied manifestations underpins the new creative ethos that powers our age.

The majority of advanced marketing positions are always advertised with the phrase "MBA preferred." While this made sense for much of the knowledge economy, it makes less sense in the creative economy. Once upon a time, the MBA was the shining beacon of the corporate hierarchy. Today, more and more that beacon is lit by the creative types who come from graphic design, copywriting, video production, and photography. Alas, the MBA is a dated badge of honor, while the creative types (many of whom hold another kind of master's degree, an MFA) are the darlings of the workplace.

What caused this shift? For one thing, MBAs are no longer different from other people in the work environment. They might not all have coding or data experience, and they might not know how to design. Many might not even know how to manipulate media to their advantage. Some aspire to strategic roles, but they don't want to execute. Laura Stack, author of *Execution Is the Strategy*, explains that when MBAs want only to strategize, both the organization and the individual fail. Stack says that "pie in the sky" strategies created by people with no boots on the ground won't succeed as often as strategies created by those who can execute for desirable results from end to end.

Geoffrey Colon
@djgeoffe

Execution is the strategy. Hire people who can think and do. You'll see more results. #disruptivefm

6:36 PM—21 Feb 2016

The disruptive marketer isn't just a 50/50 analytical/creative hybrid; he or she is also a strategy/execution/analyst expert who can do it all. And creativity is an essential skill for these roles. That's why an MFA can be more powerful than an MBA, especially if that MFA learns code!

The exciting new world of the creative economy is just the tip of a very large economic opportunity. Creatives possess new skills. And businesses want more of them because creativity isn't just a nice discipline to add to a team; it's a matter of economic life or death.

Complex, challenging creative work is difficult to automate or outsource cheaply. Indeed, creativity is what transforms utilitarian, indistinctive products like Windows 10 into devices that people actually need, love, and use creatively. Those who can transform creativity into actual disruptive execution have the potential to be the future leaders of this new world. More than ever, those with imagination are outpacing those with process.

Technology is driving this boom. Smartphones, cheap sensors, and cloud computing have enabled a raft of new Internet-connected services that are infiltrating the most tech-averse industries: Uber is roiling the taxi universe; Airbnb is disrupting the hotels industry;

Spotify has upended the music MP3 model after Napster upended the compact disc model.

In commerce, disruption is the norm and conventional brand marketing approaches won't work anymore. A business that will upend a legacy titan in the next five years probably hasn't even been born yet. But when it is, it will come from the mind of a new creative, possibly an outsider to marketing—maybe a musician or an artist who dabbles in building iOS apps.

It won't be someone armed strictly with an MBA.

RELATIONSHIP MARKETING

Let's think about how creative fields like fashion, music, and pop culture are overhauling brand marketing. Recently I've seen many articles and blogs about influencer marketing, brand advocacy, word-of-mouth marketing, and content marketing that make it appear as though these are new disciplines within marketing. Many of those who are preaching from their soapboxes are old-school marketers who only recently crossed the digital divide. It reminds me of all the newbies who think EDM (electronic dance music) was created in 2008.

Brand and marketing creativity is not new. In fact, much of it is rooted in ancient civilizations such as Mesopotamia, where one person would turn to another for goods or services. Things were so personal that rather than exchange money, most transfers were based on creative barter. The more good word of mouth a merchant could generate about his service or goods, the more able he was to feed his family.

I ran my first word-of-mouth campaign in 2003, for Red Bull Music Academy. This was prior to today's social ecosystem, and so it contained no measurements and met no ROI demands. Yet, Red Bull knew that if you excited a niche audience creatively, its members would tell their friends.

Fast-forward to today. We're in the emerging era of what author Joshua Klein has labeled "reputation economics." Essentially, according to Klein, your most powerful asset is who you know, not what you own. A combination of factors that couldn't have existed in ancient societies, or even in much of the twentieth century, gives us the ability to level the playing field, get a better idea of customers, and personalize our services while also scaling those services to a global marketplace.

For example, open-source software development is rewarded largely by peer recognition, since there is no financial reward. The desire to enhance one's reputation is the key mechanism for getting involved in such projects. Will the same lure be the case for marketing participation by customers?

The New Normal of Brand Marketing

Marketers are no longer in the advertising business; we are in the relationship business. How do we know what people are feeling before we even speak to them about a solution? In this new norm, listening—not dialoguing—is the barometer. Listening gives us an indicator of what people are feeling. These days, if you want to go out of business, keep having one-way discussions about using advertising. If you want to sustain long-term success, however, cultivate relationships by listening first and then having a dialogue in which the other party's emotional investment takes precedence.

Marketers need to spend less time advertising to their customers and more time connecting with them, growing with them, and listening to them. The path to this relationship is creativity, not knowledge. No amount of knowledge can help you in this situation.

While many companies and agencies rush to hire social media strategists, digital experts, and chief content officers, forward-thinking organizations are building influencer programs or hiring chief influencers. Some employees are simply becoming influencers without a mandate because of the abundance of publishing platforms and networks at their service, like LinkedIn, Pulse, and Medium. These programs are a combination of diagnosing customer feedback mixed with amplifying company insights in a robust, ongoing dialogue. Several of these influencers have a mixture of skills including:

- Product and competitive product awareness
- Awareness of technology evolution

- Product research and development
- People relations
- Thought leadership
- Controversial points of view

The ability to connect and listen to customers and other influencers directly within a line of business may seem antithetical to our long-held perspective on brand marketing. Yet this creative destruction uses two key elements to help customers learn and make decisions: debate and ongoing conversation.

Unfortunately, not everyone has the qualities needed to create these new programs. In the rush to be on trend with what they consider new, many organizations try to establish a foothold in a discipline in which they don't have much investment, or they will shape it to have the look and feel of an advertising campaign. We know how successful that will be.

SEEK OUT CREATIVE HYBRIDS

To navigate this new, creative economic growth territory, the best way to be a marketer is to not be a marketer at all. Instead, it is to be a media company. For years, media companies struggled with digital formats, but lately they seem to be crossing the chasm. The *New York Times, Washington Post,* and even Condé Nast have embraced new ways of thinking. Armed with content, data, and creative talent, BuzzFeed, Vox, Mashable, and many new media outlets have successfully pushed the envelope, reimagining what media should look and feel like. And the titans have perked up. As of July 30, 2015, NBC/Universal was heavily invested in both BuzzFeed and Vox. Even big media legacies realize the power of data-driven, creative-hybrid outlets.

While brands continue to navigate this new world, it's important to note who is on your team and how the team handles working in this environment. So, ditch the "MBAs preferred" approach to marketing and embrace the 50/50 creative-hybrid approach. You can start by building on and improving these seven personality traits for your team:

1. **Listening skills.** Listening is essential to future success. To truly find out what's interesting in the world and how it links with other things, you need to possess amazing listening skills. This flies in the face of conventional marketing, which has always believed in amplification. Yet as we know, those who do all the talking cannot stay silent long enough to listen and learn. Know when to shut up.

2. **Curiosity.** Rather than trying to find something interesting in everything, pay attention to the things you *genuinely* find interesting—no matter how obscure, silly, embarrassing, or irrelevant they may seem. Because when you are curious, you bring your whole self to whatever you're doing. You give it your full attention, and you have the energy and persistence you need to do something innovative.

CASE IN POINT
Think Like Da Vinci

You can be curious about more than one thing at a time. Author and entrepreneur Frans Johansson has dubbed this "The Medici Effect": "When you step into an intersection of fields, disciplines, or cultures, you can combine existing concepts into a large number of extraordinary new ideas." Leonardo da Vinci is often revered as a universal genius, equally at home in the arts, sciences, and engineering. Steve Jobs and the late, great advertising guru David Ogilvy are frequently thought of in the same way.

In da Vinci's time, the conventional separations between disciplines did not exist, as they currently do in corporate or academic environments. Universalism was an attribute common to all gifted persons of the Renaissance, not unique to Leonardo. Sort of reminds you of a liberal arts education, right?

da Vinci moved easily from science to art and back again. Only in a culture in which there were no rigid boundaries could this take place. This is the world where the generalist now lives in business.

Alas, there are too many people in positions of power who don't like the lack of single-minded focus that's prevalent among the "butterfly minds" of today's Internet generation. But perhaps this is not a hideous modern aberration so much as a return to the world of Leonardo da Vinci, where it was considered normal, even admirable, to flit from one thing to another. da Vinci's notebooks are full of half-baked projects, such as flying machines that literally never got off the ground. But nobody seemed to get upset about that.

Geoffrey Colon
@djgeoffe

Curiosity is the number one trait in a disruptive marketer. Hire people who ask "what if?" #disruptivefm

6:37 PM — 21 Feb 2016

---

3. **Emotional Intelligence.** I believe that a greater awareness of emotional intelligence (EI) will lead to more women taking positions of power in marketing and in embracing disruptive marketing. Some industries are becoming so competitive that effective marketing is no longer a numbers game. Instead, it is about connecting with customers and clients in meaningful ways. This connecting entails building friendships with your target audience so they adopt your culture. Those entrepreneurs who can successfully walk in the shoes of their customers almost always create a foolproof model for success and longevity.

4. **Creativity.** Steve Jobs famously said,

> Creativity is just connecting things. When you ask creative people how they did something, they feel a little guilty because they didn't really do it. They just saw something. It seemed obvious to them after a while; that's because they were able to connect experiences they've had and synthesize new things. And the reason they were able to do that was that they've had more experiences or they have thought more about their experiences than other people. Unfortunately, that's

too rare a commodity. A lot of people in our industry
haven't had very diverse experiences.

In the creative economy, every profession requires some
degree of creativity. Creativity is taking preexisting elements
and integrating them in a way that has never been done
before, with the aim of improving conditions. Indeed, some
may argue that creativity is the source of all innovations and
improvements. And how you build that creative vision is
through experience. How you gain experience is by doing
as many different things as possible. You never know how
those experiences will influence the future.

5. **Abundance.** In the book *Free: The Future of a Radical Price*,
Chris Anderson counts the ways that giving away content
can help boost your business and build your tribe. He
argues that many individuals under the age of thirty aren't
used to paying for digital information when they know they
can find it somewhere online for free. By tapping into this
demand for getting something for nothing, you can attract
and maintain a loyal audience while building premiums
as you go. Some feel this flies in the face of monetization.
Again, a growth hacker builds via customer experience,
whereas an MBA-trained brand marketer uses monetization. The former is thinking about the customer; the latter
is thinking simply about the company.

6. **Story making.** Marketing is no longer about corporate storytelling, mind tactics, manipulation, or persuasion. It's
about inspiring your audience to tell a story by using media
in new and different forms. Ask yourself, "What story does
my business allow others to build or make? How do they
help translate a narrative with their POV to others?"

7. **Generalist experts.** If you're a marketer and still don't
understand how paid social targeting works, you should
make an effort to improve your knowledge and skill set in
this area. If you're good with pay-per-click advertising and
data, but you don't understand the creative process that
goes into producing video, creating imagery, or design,
make an effort to learn more about how creative content is

[handwritten margin note: story making. not telling]

actually made. Don't be an expert in one area. Be an expert in both.

In 2013, during a Twitter chat session, I noted that social marketing and search marketing were rapidly fusing. When people asked why I thought this, I noted two converging data patterns:

1. Search advertising is set up around keyword and segmentation targeting to serve your ad. When a user clicks on an ad because she feels it's relevant, the advertiser tracks convergence and the network the ad is served on builds revenue. Facebook and Twitter are similar to Google and Bing in these areas.

2. Ultimately, social networks are integrating search into their offerings to create a frictionless user experience. For example, I might not want to toggle between two applications in order to Google something while I am on Facebook or Twitter if I can perform the search right there. Plus, in the near future, search options may center on interests, not keywords.

For those in the marketing profession, it's not enough anymore to be "just a creative" or "just a data scientist." You now have to be a generalist. For a number of professions, the world is converging. Even education has adopted hybrid modeling, where students learn more because they choose subject matters to learn on their own—and this kind of "active learning" results in better test performance and what is known as subject mastery (or subject knowledge).

The key to success lies in understanding how all these technologies intersect with creativity. You can't be a subject-matter expert in only one field. You have to be a generalist. *You have to be a hybrid professional.*

My wife, Allison, said it best when she entered the world of digital video content after working in television production for ten years. When I asked her why some people who had twenty years' experience were being passed over for an open senior role at her company, she said, "They are looking for a *preditor* hybrid for that position."

"A what? Sounds like a machine from *The Terminator*. How does that help in digital content?"

She laughed. "Not a predator, a preditor, a 'Producer/Editor.'"

What she meant by this was someone who can shoot, produce, and edit content. The reason they had a hard time finding someone is many candidates with the execution experience don't have the managerial skills, while many of those with managerial experience don't have the execution skills!

There's a reason hybrid roles are picking up steam. Companies always want to cut costs, but they also want people who understand entire processes so as to create efficiencies. These new hybrid roles offer agility at the same time as they peel away layers of bureaucracy (freeing up more space for creative thinking!).

In conventional marketing, you may have hired one person to do search engine optimization, another to do search engine marketing, another to build and design a website, another to do social media, and yet another to do inbound marketing. A disruptive marketer is a hybrid professional who can do all those things while analyzing web and social analytics to figure out what landing page has the highest bounce rate and what video to shoot for Snapchat tomorrow.

The disruptive marketer figures out what tools work best in any particular scenario. It's not a matter of either/or. It's a matter of what if? In an era in which creativity may be the main motivation to provide customer connection, we need more tinkerers. Is the 1950s "organization man" finally behind us? Bruce Nussbaum, author of *Creative Intelligence*, thinks so. "The organization man is dead," he writes. "He thrived when smokestack America thrived. When airlines, banks and telephone companies were highly regulated. When Japan built shoddy cars. When computers were huge and an apple was something you ate." Good riddance.

PART II
THE NEW
PERSONALITY OF
MARKETING SUCCESS

CHAPTER 5

THE DISRUPTIVE MARKETER'S MINDSET
Punk Rocker, New Parent, Soccer Player

> One thing I like about jazz is that it emphasized doing things
> differently from what other people were doing.
>
> —HERBIE HANCOCK, jazz pianist

THE AVERAGE POP song clocks in at about three minutes and twenty
seconds (3:20). How do I know this? Well, for one, a Bing search
indicates that the average time a pop song is played on FM radio
is between three and four minutes. Pull a cross section of about a
hundred current pop music videos on YouTube and you will find
they range from 2:40 to 3:59. Crunching the data, you find that the
average time lands somewhere between 2:40 and 4:00, or around
3:20. That's how long an artist has to convince you to download the
song from iTunes or to open Spotify.

Divide that time by ten, and you get twenty seconds, which, according to the most recent study I could find, is the amount of time
that most people actually spend watching a video. For videos, after
the first twenty seconds, audience engagement wanes.

Now let's think like a disruptive marketer and ask, "What if it isn't
a pop song? What if it's hardcore punk?" Now we're thinking differently. And in fact, twenty seconds is the perfect amount of time
in which to make a point with a hardcore punk song, which can say
everything it needs to in one minute or less. In addition, in a live
setting there are distractions galore (stage diving, mosh pits, utter

chaos) that prevent the audience from truly giving its undivided attention to any one thing.

Sounds a lot like modern life, right?

CASES IN POINT
Go with the Flow

In 1986, when I was fourteen years old, my older brother Brian took me to a hardcore punk rock show in Catasauqua, Pennsylvania, where I witnessed many one-minute songs. One of the bands that night was Raw Power, from Italy. I remember someone handing me a fanzine (a fan magazine, the equivalent of a digital-era blog) and another person handing me a flyer urging me to tune in to 91.3 FM, WLVR, a local, noncommercial radio station, every Thursday night from 9 to 11 PM for a hardcore punk radio show (comparable to a modern-day podcast).

This event was very different from the "concerts" I had read so much about in *Hit Parader* magazine, which featured big arena bands like Van Halen and Mötley Crüe. After watching the performance, I noted that there was no real barrier between the band and the audience. After playing nonstop for sixty sweaty minutes, Raw Power's drummer stood up and began breaking down his kit to load it into the van. There was no drum tech or "roadie."

This was a pure scene. Participants loved the music and were passionate about the bands. They approached this world with a "Do It Yourself," or DIY, ethos. DIY didn't exist in the corporate music world; bands relied on the label machine to make them a hit. Nor does it exist in today's corporate business world, where too many companies rely on conventional marketers to convince customers to adopt poor products.

I remained fascinated with the hardcore punk scene for much of my teen years, mainly because, unlike other musical movements, anyone could be a part of it. It broke down the silos and hierarchies to which we often cling for safety in an uncertain world. And this DIY attitude among the participants allowed bands to form from nothing— and teenage promoters to put on shows anywhere. It allowed people with no broadcasting background to host and present college radio shows, and for seven- and twelve-inch vinyl records to be pressed by people with no record label experience. The scene allowed bands to become part of your life.

Geoffrey Colon
@djgeoffe

Customers have the ability to do anything now, including your advertising. #disruptivefm

2:25 AM — 3 Mar 2016

Fast-forward twenty-three years to 2009. It's after midnight on July 26 in Park Slope, Brooklyn. Allison and I had just returned home from a long walk after seeing a movie. It was one of those hot, humid nights in the city when it seems impossible to get cool even in an air-conditioned movie theater.

Allison was eight months pregnant. We were expecting our first child in about two weeks. But life had other plans. Allison thought her water had broken. Around 12:35 AM she phoned the doctor on call, who suggested we come to the hospital just to be extra safe.

We hadn't planned for this; Allison hadn't even packed her overnight bag. We were such amateurs! Instead of trying to control the situation, we approached it with an agile mindset and took the actions we deemed necessary based on the context. The Manhattan Bridge was closed for repairs, so we took the Brooklyn Bridge to the Upper West Side of Manhattan. Allison gave birth to a beautiful baby girl we named Olive. Then the real fun began, and we realized that despite all the books we had read and all the parents we had spoken with, parenting is pretty much about learning on your feet and dealing with whatever life throws at you.

Another way I learned on my feet (literally speaking) was through the beautiful game of soccer (you may call it football or futbol depending on your part of the world). Rewinding to the year 1978, I recall kicking my first soccer ball in a competitive game at age six. The game excited me because it never stopped. The ball was constantly in motion, which meant my body was constantly moving to keep pace. Where would the ball go next? Where would I go with the ball if it came to me? When you receive a pass, you have so little time to decide what to do next. As a result, soccer is as much a mental game as it is a physical one.

Now at age forty-four, and living in Seattle, I still play soccer and show no signs of slowing down or stopping. Success in a game like soccer requires a hybrid set of skills. One of the most important is the ability to think on your feet. You have to know what to do with the ball, and then perform that action with precision. There are no set plays when the ball is in motion.

BLUEPRINT FOR SUCCESS: A HYBRID SKILL SET

Hardcore punk is a blueprint for communication today. That is, people interested in the subject now drive the messages. Instead of anyone being able to start a band or a fanzine, now anyone can initiate a podcast or a blog. These Do-It-Yourselfers are a brand's participatory customers. New parenting, too, is a blueprint for how business now operates. But instead of dealing with a fickle newborn, you've got to figure out how to reach fickle—and mobile—customers.

Geoffrey Colon
@djgeoffe

There are no timeouts in soccer, just like there are no timeouts in customer relationship management.
#disruptivefm

2:39 AM — 29 Feb 2016

Soccer, in fact, is a blueprint for how marketing operates today. Instead of timeouts and planning sessions, modern marketers need to think on their feet in real time to keep up with the demands of customers and the marketplace.

Successful marketing no longer requires only one set of skills. In fact, some of the skills that once made marketers successful are actually detrimental. Age and tenure used to be badges of honor; today experience means little, as new trends and behaviors come and go daily.

While planning for the next year used to help in reaching a firm's objectives, now when business is done changes all the time—marketing isn't limited to a nine-to-five, Monday-to-Friday schedule. In fact, disruptive marketers know the best time to reach consumers is during the evening or on weekends, when they have downtime and are more likely to be in the mood to learn about and immerse themselves in your content. Yet, conventional marketers still operate when it's most comfortable for them, without thinking about their customers' lifestyles and habits.

I used to ask the hardcore punk bands, "Why did you form your band?" Many said that they simply wanted to try something different. (Note to self: try something different!) When Allison was expecting the baby, like other expectant and new parents I was always afraid that I'd do something wrong. New parents are constantly second guessing themselves. When I asked other parents about this, many told me I would simply learn how to adapt, based on the situation. (Note to self: adapt to the situation!)

When I ask soccer players why they enjoy the sport, most say (as I do), "There's always something happening and you have to adjust your strategy in real time in order to be competitive." (Note to self: think on your feet in real time!)

Lately, when I speak to marketers, all too often I am asked, "Will what you are suggesting work?" As someone looking to push the boundaries by executing more disruptive marketing, my answer is, "What's your definition of success?" If the person can't answer that, he or she shouldn't even be in the business.

If you only do things when you know the answers in advance, your marketing won't be very interesting and your company will simply fade away.

THE CULTURE OF DISRUPTION:
TEST, MEASURE, ADVANCE

A disruptive marketer understands first and foremost that the creation of new ideas from intimate data analysis is what ultimately helps form the benchmarks against which to test and measure. Measurement gives you the ability to map your next steps. And your next steps move you forward with new product innovation, new ways to engage, new ways to use that engagement, thereby understanding and solving the new business mysteries with new solutions.

This is disruptive because for much of the twentieth century marketing was seen as a strategic investment. Companies did it because they felt they had to. There wasn't much need for measuring results. In the twenty-first century, though, we have greater ability to gather, analyze, and act on data. Almost all disruptive marketing activities in some way enable testing and measuring.

Geoffrey Colon
@djgeoffe

If you don't measure your marketing, how do you expect to improve your output over time? #disruptivefm

6:39 PM—21 Feb 2016

This measurement means disruptive marketers, while relying heavily on creativity to stand out, must also depend on metrics to see if their tactics are helping them meet their objectives.

You should never say, "I think our advertising is working because profits are up." Rather, you should say, "Forty-five percent of our content marketing initiatives drove leads that converted to $300 million in quarter one because we identified that our audience enjoys hip-hop, so we created a piece of entertainment with Nas in the content."

To many of us, this is a new space, just as it was for those hard-core punk bands that were experimenting in 1986. Of course in 1992, a band from Seattle named Nirvana appeared to come out of nowhere with a brash sound many had never heard before. Nirvana was credited with altering the American pop-music landscape, although the sound was anything but new. It sprang from almost fifteen years of innovation by hundreds of bands that remained below the radar. Nevertheless, Nirvana got to carry a flag.

Though the outlier bands never got rich or found wider audiences, they did spawn a small but sprawling network of bands, labels, fanzines, radio stations, and other subversive collective systems that helped reenergize American rock, giving it a DIY credo and producing a music that was deeply personal, emotional, challenging, and influential.

Disruptive marketers can learn from those early innovators about the importance of a DIY ethos to the creation of new marketing models and processes. In other words, we should all be acting like young punk rockers, constantly establishing new "scenes" while overthrowing old "systems."

Similarly, we should be acting like new parents, taking things as they come and figuring out the solutions. While plans are wonderful, plans have to change because the externals around us change.

Our new world is both abundant and inattentive; therefore, we have to take more risks now. Disruptive and DIY movements pressure organizations to go beyond the norm, forcing them to diverge from the crowd, requiring them to blaze new paths in a world ruled by habits, hierarchy, hindsight bias, and normalcy.

The Shared Vision Meme Myth

Where does *normalcy* in business originate? And how does the disruptive marketer avoid getting caught in its trap? Much of normalcy comes from what is known as the "shared vision meme."

Most companies assume that there is only one single and defined vision for the organization. This vision comes from its founder, the CEO, or upper management. It is expected that the rest of the organization will accept this vision and march to the same drummer.

Geoffrey Colon
@djgeoffe

The shared vision meme in business only creates more conformity. Business is about being different, not creating a cult. #disruptivefm

6:40 PM—21 Feb 2016

We often read about the shared vision meme in the business sections of large news outlets. The *New York Times* wrote about Amazon CEO and founder Jeff Bezos, defining a cultural revolution at his company that was complete with laminated rules on how employees should behave. This was being done in the belief that rules push employees to lean in toward group-think and conformity, since it leaves no room for interpretation.

The disruptive world has an opposing view: having set principles makes an organization rigid and inflexible. And that's the total opposite of the young punk rocker or DIY ethos. In reality, the highest-performing organizations actively promote dissent and flexibility in all areas, including product development and marketing. Unfortunately, not many companies subscribe to this ideology. I can name only a handful: Red Bull, Virgin Group, T-Mobile, Tesla, American Express, Google, and IBM. (Note: I didn't mention Microsoft, Facebook, or Apple because although they build and develop extraordinary products, they use conventional marketing strategies.)

Companies such as Red Bull, Virgin Group, and T-Mobile don't treat their employees as "resources," "assets," or "roles"; these characterizations dehumanize people and make robots of them. Robots don't create thinking, feeling, emotionally driven stories, and they don't build identifiable cultures that customers crave. In an uncertain, rapidly changing business world, making safe bets won't provide much movement. Calculated risks don't open up the eyes of customers looking for different products, innovative packaging, constant product updates, or left-of-center experiences.

While the theme of this book is that thinking and acting differently is the differentiating factor in marketing, I acknowledge that you probably don't want to take risks. After all, companies that don't take risks benefit most by staying the course. Right? Maybe not . . .

Let's take a quick look at the top five U.S. companies, as rated by their employees:

1. Google
2. Bain & Company
3. Nestle Purina PetCare Company
4. F5 Networks
5. Boston Consulting Group

Now let's list the top five companies based on market valuation:

1. Apple
2. Exxon Mobil
3. Berkshire Hathaway
4. Google
5. Microsoft

And the top five most innovative companies based on customer event experiences:

1. Bud Light
2. Nike
3. American Express
4. Microsoft
5. iHeart Radio

Finally, here are the five most popular products based on consumption:

1. Coca-Cola
2. Lay's Potato Chips
3. PlayStation
4. Toyota Corolla
5. Apple iPad

Next, let's cross-match these lists and note which companies appear on two or more. There are only three: Google, Microsoft, and Apple.

Those companies are among the highest valued, so it makes sense that their employees rank them high, their customers rank them high, and their products are bought in large quantities.

Now, let's look a little deeper and ask a "what if" question. What if we looked at the top five valuated companies by market capitalization in 2015 again? Here's the list:

1. Apple
2. Exxon Mobil
3. Berkshire Hathaway
4. Google
5. Microsoft

Now, how about that same list in 2006?

1. Exxon Mobil
2. General Electric
3. Microsoft
4. Citigroup
5. Gazprom

Geoffrey Colon

@djgeoffe

Only 2 of the top 5 valued companies by market capitalization in 2006 are still top 5 today. #disruptivefm

9:13 PM — 28 Feb 2016

The historical data shows that energy companies have a whole set of new circumstances they will need to solve in order to remain relevant. Meanwhile, technology companies that enable us with communications are beginning to dominate the list, with even more companies forming in the tech sector as I write this. What great leaps of risk will these new companies bring to the new normal? Will these leaps be from a shared vision of group-think or involve bets against the status quo?

Look back at the 2015 top-five list. What if these companies don't take risks moving forward the next ten years? Will they be on the list in 2026?

Risk to Learn

There is no real cause for failure in this new world of marketing. There are only things we can learn. There is more data available than ever before to pivot or pursue in real time with messaging, content, and experiences. Failure occurs for those who persevere on pride even when the customer user experience data informs them they should have concluded their experiment months ago. Some schools of thought welcome risk because trends are emerging and transforming at such a fast pace that there are more unknowns than knowns in the business world. We can learn from failure in marketing, but only if marketing involves everyone, not just the marketing department, as shown next.

Geoffrey Colon
@djgeoffe

There is no failure in this new world of marketing. Only learning. #disruptivefm

8:50 PM—7 Mar 2016

THE NEUROSCIENCE OF SCREWING UP

In 2009, *Wired* magazine featured an article entitled "Accept Defeat: The Neuroscience of Screwing Up" that addressed this very issue. In it, author Jonah Lehrer talked about how two lab teams were given the same problem. One of the teams was made up of single-subject experts; the other was people with different backgrounds and expertise. Which group do you think solved the problem more efficiently?

The group of single-subject experts took weeks to solve the problem by using a traditional method involving tests of various approaches. The diverse group solved the problem in *ten minutes* in an informal group meeting.

What lesson can we draw from this? For one thing, teams of "experts and insiders" can be marketing's worst enemy. Because they believe there is only one approach to finding a solution, they tend not to accept outlying ideas. When marketing teams represent a cross section of disciplines, the problems are quickly solved and the solutions are often applicable to other areas of business as well. One reason industries are being overthrown is that they don't allow outsiders into their inner circle to provide new ways of thinking.

The *Wired* article got to the root of what I'm discussing in this chapter. Marketing is about communication—but it's not communication with people who look, dress, and think in the same way. To succeed in this new era of marketing, you've got to think and act like a punk rocker. You have to invite everyone to the party who wants to be part of something big. You have to stop thinking like an MBA in a suit and tie and instead dress down, simplify, and realize that everyone has some tools to help you with your marketing.

You need to find people who aren't like you, and be inspired by the things they say, even if those things are weird. Indeed, outsiders shock us out of our cognitive boxes. To succeed in this future world of widely available free information, you have to escape the cookie-cutter mindset. You have to think like a prospect, a customer, or the target audience you wish to persuade and inspire.

The moment you place yourself outside the company and—from an empathetic viewpoint—think about how your products, services, and communications will be accepted by others, things will change. This is why it's so critical that you uproot the tangles of your professional life every two years. You never want to get too comfortable in one position for too long.

CASE IN POINT
The Cereal CEO of the Music Industry

In the mid-1990s, while I was working in the music business, several changes occurred in the industry. Among them were that big multinational music companies were letting go of their CEOs and replacing them with leaders from outside the industry. This action caught many off guard. They asked, "What does an executive who marketed cereal know about the music industry?" Many thought it was a stupid move.

Now, what if I gave you a bicycle that turned right every time you steered it to the left? Could you ride it? That is what Dustin Wilson Sandlin—engineer and producer of YouTube channel "Smarter Everyday"—did to see if he could retrain his brain. Sandlin practiced for eight months until he could ride the "backwards brain bicycle." And what do you think happened when he went back to a normal bike? He had to relearn how to ride it!

Here's the takeaway from this experiment. We have an innate bias in our decision making. To break away from this, we need to retrain or relearn how we view the world. Much of that job comes from taking what's known in marketing as a "design thinking" approach.

DESIGN THINKING IN
DISRUPTIVE MARKETING

Tim Brown, author of *Change by Design*, describes *design thinking* as using designer skills to match people's needs with market opportunity. The goal of design thinking is to reach an improved future state. In this regard, it's a form of solution-based or solution-focused thinking: starting with a goal (a better future situation) instead of trying to solve a specific problem.

This approach differs from the analytical scientific method, which begins with a statement of the problem by defining all the parameters in order to create a solution. The design-thinking process stresses the "building up" of ideas, with few or no limits during a brainstorming phase. This freedom of thought reduces the participants' fears of failure and encourages varied participation in idea creation. Think of it as a brainstorming session on steroids.

Hire More Generalists, Fewer Experts

The phrase "thinking outside the box" was coined to describe the brainstorming session. The practice aids in the discovery of hidden elements, ambiguities, and potential faulty assumptions.

Geoffrey Colon
@djgeoffe

Hire generalists who can learn lots of things very quickly and enjoy conducting marketing experiments. #disruptivefm

7:08 PM—21 Feb 2016

So, if you're a team leader who is a specialist, don't hire only people like you. Hire generalists who can learn quickly a number of subject matter areas and who enjoy conducting marketing experiments. This is exactly what the music industry did in 1992. It was asking the "what if" question about transitioning from an era in which music moguls ruled the business to a new period with a global perspective. In the 1970s and 1980s, it was totally acceptable for a company to sign and ship music strictly within the United States. If margins were low, it was easy to make a profit. Yet in the 1990s, with the passage of NAFTA and other global trade measures (as noted by Thomas L. Friedman in his book *The World Is Flat*), there was suddenly a global marketplace with multiple audiences and wider opportunities.

Although in the twenty-first century it will be commonplace for professionals from one industry to take jobs in other industries, as mentioned earlier, twenty years ago such moves were considered anathema. Traditionalists in the music industry hated this management move, but many of those outsiders came with new ways of thinking, new processes, and new efficiencies.

In any business, people spend a long time learning about a particular specialty, with the goal of becoming an expert in that field. Usually we do this because we are rewarded for that expertise. In the music industry's heyday, being an executive who signed enough artists who sold lots of records meant you worked your way up from an associate to VP, and ultimately to executive VP. You might even have been anointed president.

The troubling thing about becoming an expert, though, is that we become entrenched. We put on blinders, rendering us unable to see anything beyond what is happening directly in front of us. This makes sense from a biological perspective; as humans, we find it easier to partake in implementation thinking, which is the ability to organize ideas and plans in a way that they will be effectively carried out.

Implementation thinking, which is tactical, is the crutch of conventional marketers. Entrepreneur and philanthropist Naveen Jain, founder of the World Innovation Institute, doesn't believe in expert theory:

> I believe that people who will come up with creative solutions to solve the world's biggest problems . . . will NOT be experts in their fields. The real disruptors will be those individuals who are not steeped in one industry of choice, with those coveted 10,000 hours of experience, but instead, individuals who approach challenges with a clean lens, bringing together diverse experiences, knowledge and opportunities.

Ask Yourself: What Could Be Possible?

If you expect to be deeply personal, emotional, challenging, and influential—like those early innovative hardcore punk bands that came before Nirvana—you need to push your boundaries. Being smack-dab in the middle of your industry doesn't bode well for coming up with new ideas. That's because your assumptions and inherent biases will always get in the way. Your thinking will be more transactional than conceptual, innovative, or intuitive. And it's conceptual, innovative, and intuitive thinking that will move you ahead.

Geoffrey Colon
@djgeoffe

Experts won't help your marketing as much as outside forces like non-traditional fields. #disruptivefm

7:16 PM—21 Feb 2016

Before we move on to the next chapter, where I showcase how "tinkering" thinking can help build some of the best marketing ideas and movements, ask yourself this question: "What *could* be possible in my industry?" Not what *is* possible, or what *will* be possible, but what *could* be possible. Then ask, "If it does become possible, how do I market that future state?"

Here's an example you can apply to your business: the smartphone and its search capabilities. Consider these five true statements:

1. I can search anywhere on a smartphone with or without a Wi-Fi connection.
2. I can use a mobile browser like Safari to conduct a keyword search.
3. I can use applications like Twitter, YouTube, Instagram, or LinkedIn to conduct deeper vertical searches that go beyond keywords into particular fields of interest or for assets.
4. I can use Siri, Cortana, or Google Now to ask a voice-enabled search that will generate answers.
5. I can use near field communication (NFC) applications like Shazam to generate answers to questions by listening to what is around me.

Many of us use only the first two features on that list, but some of us use all five. Yet, if we are expecting to innovate our mobile marketing around technology and human behavior, and we are blinded by the current stars of our industry, what are the chances we'll come up with something new? It's going to be much harder than we may think, because our point of view is clouded by what we know—the familiar—which prejudices our judgment, just as those classic record music industry moguls were blind to innovation possibilities.

With that in mind, let's generate a list of what *could* be possible to reimagine in this one industry sector:

- I could search from a watch or glasses, or in the near future, any touch-enabled, "smart" glass surface, extending my smartphone into other sectors of the world.
- I could search based on my behavior history from wearable devices that provide information without my having to enter keywords into a search box. My smartphone will send me reminders.
- I could search based on software that knows what I'm feeling, turning my smartphone into a mood detector.
- I could search based on location or beacon technology that knows where I am, knows what I like based on my searches and social signals, and sends me things that I may enjoy. Now my smartphone is a sensory detector.
- I could search based on my physical health and what I'm ingesting. My smartphone becomes a health and wellness improvement center.

The biggest problem facing marketers today is that we've all been trained to think too much like marketers. As a first step in a new direction, consider inviting outsiders to help develop ideas—people who aren't hampered by the same assumptions as you have. Mind you, these are not focus groups; these are not question-and-answer sessions with customers. These are brainstorming sessions with people from diverse backgrounds.

Mike Street, a close friend from the marketing world and producer of the SmartBrownVoices.com podcast, drives the following point home; it can help us all in our quest to reshape marketing:

I started my podcast, SmartBrownVoices.com, as a direct response to the lack of people of color [to whom] the media will talk . . . about marketing, PR, and digital growth. When I look at sites like GrowthHackers.tv, . . . of 153 interviews, there are no brown people. We work in this space and have big success, but no one wants to talk to us. And while people of color over-index on social platforms, the social "experts" that everyone talks to all look the same. So if your voice isn't heard, you're basically hiding. Social media has allowed everyone to be heard and to find those who will listen.

There are voices everywhere, and they all have a point of view. Listen to them.

Now that we've reimagined the role of a marketer in the twenty-first century, let us begin to understand how fringe activities eventually become movements. The best place to analyze this is from the vantage point of the DJ, thereby discovering how tinkering with two turntables can reveal new ways to enhance your marketing.

CHAPTER 6

THE GENIUS OF TINKERERS AND "TEMPORARY" MARKETERS

*Change is inevitable, and when it happens, the wisest response
is not to wail or whine but to suck it up and deal with it.*

—DANIEL H. PINK, *A Whole New Mind: Why Right Brainers Will Rule the Future*

IN THE LATE nineteenth and early twentieth centuries, large bands
and orchestras performed most popular music. Beginning in the
1950s, things changed. Now, four or five individuals came together
and formed a rock band. Then in the late 1970s, the DIY punk
ethos shook things up, and anyone could pick up a guitar and
form a band.

Geoffrey Colon
@djgeoffe

What at one time had to be performed by a 20-person
band can now be done by one DJ. It's the same with
marketing. #disruptivefm

2:47 AM — 29 Feb 2016

While some young, revolutionary artists were picking up guitars, others picked up synthesizers, whittling down a four-member band to two people on stage—usually a vocalist and a synth player. Via sampling and sequencing technology, they could re-create all the sounds of a band themselves. If you think the way music was performed would stop at that two-person band, though, you are incorrect. Today, DJs on stage play prerecorded music.

In the same way as the art of DJing changed popular music, the disruptive marketer will forever change how marketing operates. This will happen by ushering in analytics, design, and philosophy in place of MBAs, brand marketers, and traditional business studies. You see, the best movements never really begin as movements. They begin when great minds begin tinkering to find solutions to problems that challenge them.

If I had to pick one DJ who tinkered above the rest, I'd head back to the borough that housed the studios of WEAF-AM and that ultimately gave birth to DJing as an art form. That borough is the Bronx. That DJ is Grandmaster Flash.

Born Joseph Saddler in 1958, Grandmaster Flash is considered the pioneer of modern-day hip-hop DJing. And Saddler was the ultimate "tinkerer." He studied many other DJs and began to experiment with some of the skills he saw them using to produce entirely new creations.

What was Saddler's most important creation? The backspin technique. The DJ plays the record on one turntable at a normal number of beats per minute (BPM), and then quickly spins the record backward to create a whirlwind effect; then, using a mixing board to toggle between the two audio sources, he bumps over to the beat of a new track on the second turntable.

When Grandmaster Flash combined this trick with another called scratching (originally invented by Grand Wizzard Theodore), his DJ sets took on a performance aspect that had previously not existed in the world of DJing. He made the DJ a performer, not just a human jukebox.

Instead of playing a record, cueing a record, and playing another record, Flash formed an entirely new idea based on a platform of ideas that had come before him. In fact, he embraced and took tinkering to a whole new level.

TINKERING AS A STRATEGY

Saddler's innovative spirit of tinkering can be applied to marketing. Let's say your organization is debating whether to do a search advertising campaign or a social media campaign. If the discussion boils down to an either/or choice, well, you're not tinkering enough. The tinkering mind would use *both* solutions. They are complementary, not at odds. The social helps capture awareness, while the search captures the intent generated from that awareness. If your marketing has been reduced to templates and scorecards, with a rigid structure and no means to draw outside the lines, you're not tinkering.

Tracking your spending is important, of course. You have to know where the best place is to invest your marketing dollars. However, allocate at least 10 percent of your marketing budget for campaigns with a zero ROI. These experiments will help you identify future trends, so ultimately you do get ROI. It's a lot easier to test on a small scale now (even if you can't track every expenditure) than it is to play catch-up later.

Alec Foege, author of *The Tinkerers: The Amateurs, DIYers, and Inventors Who Make America Great*, best explained tinkering in the world of marketing in a 2012 piece for *Salon*:

> At its most basic level, tinkering is making something genuinely new out of the things that already surround us. Secondly, tinkering is something that happens without an initial sense of purpose, or at least with a purpose quite different from the one originally identified. Tinkering also emanates from a place of passion or obsession. Lastly, tinkering is a disruptive act in which the tinkerer pivots from history and begins a new journey that results in innovation, invention, and illumination.

So again, I ask you a question: When was the last time you tinkered when developing a marketing plan?

CASE IN POINT

No Money? Creative Problem-Solving

My tinkering story began in 1991, when my college roommate carted me ninety miles away to a club in midtown Manhattan. When we arrived, I realized this was not going to be any normal night out, in the conventional sense. The club was an old church that had been outfitted with Roboscan intelligent lighting and a bass-heavy sound system. The scene was part circus, part concert, part science fiction film set, and part laboratory, all morphed into one.

Entering the main chapel, we found the music was loud, pulsing and throbbing with repetitive beats. It being 1991, the music was programmed by DJs using two turntables to mix and blend the beats. As I watched the DJ mix records for almost four hours, I wondered what it would be like to mix two different forms of sound together and create a whole new sound. This is what Grandmaster Flash brought to the world of DJing. He made something that was formulaic and mechanical into a new art form. Because I had adopted a DIY ethos from my years in the punk scene, I asked myself, "What if I tried to do this?"

I questioned my roommate for more information about the music the DJs were programming. "It's called house music!" he shouted loudly over the piercing throb on the main floor. I decided then and there to find out where this house music was being built. I found out later that house music, an African American invention from Chicago, was mainly a fixture in big cities. It was programmed by DJs at events that didn't use conventional advertising to attract audiences. Unlike other forms of music, in which artists were the main promotional vehicles, these DJs were the fixtures on the scene, many of whom toured globally.

The main instrument for spreading this sound was the cassette mixtape, which could be dubbed and redubbed, and shared among others interested in the music. (Sounds a lot like social media platforms in the organic sense, no?)

When I got back to Lehigh University, I found a person selling two high-end Technics 1200-MK2 turntables for $300 each. Since $600 was out of my price range, I bartered my design services for the turn-tables. I also purchased a cheap mixer for $35 at Radio Shack and got to work. A huge vinyl aficionado, I had plenty of music to mix. The question was how to mix it so as to create something new.

YouTube didn't exist yet, so I spent much of my time the next year watching DJs perform in every club I could get into. I took what I witnessed and tried to copy it while adding my own touches. As with any repeat exercise, I got better over time. Eventually I decided to put together my first mixtape. The entire time I was doing this I wasn't thinking about ROI; I was simply thinking about rapid growth and influence.

That first mixtape was special. It included various types of music and musical influences. And it was different because I used a lot of hip-hop DJ tricks on genres other than house music—such as rock, electro, and punk; these usually weren't cut and mixed on turntables. While my goal was to give the mixtape to anyone who wanted to listen to it, the bigger goal was to post an audio of it on the World Wide Web so early adopters could find it and help me get paid gigs.

Then one day I spotted a classified ad in a local newspaper for a loft space in Allentown, Pennsylvania, that was available for private parties. Rather than trying to work my way up the club hierarchy, I decided to growth-hack my way there by combining my graphic design skills to create a flyer and my DJ skills to host a big party.

There was risk involved. Who would attend? I could lose my initial investment, a $1,000 rental fee and 80 percent of the net door pro-ceeds. So, I went back to the loft owner and negotiated this deal: if he gave me $2 out of the $5 I was planning to charge, I would sign the contract. My thinking was this: if five hundred people came, I would have $1,000 in my pocket to pay the rental fee. He said it was a deal.

I got to work duplicating about one hundred mixtapes with my phone number on them. I would charge $5 for each so as to make a profit from the gig. If I got word of mouth going about myself, that would drive mind share and help me with future bookings.

> **Geoffrey Colon**
> @djgeoffe
>
> ---
>
> Disruptive marketers work with no resources. Lack of resources actually helps develop their creative problem-solving skills. #disruptivefm
>
> ---
>
> 2:35 AM—3 Mar 2016

We'll stop the story here. I don't need to explain the outcome or what happened in the next five years. The point is that when I started tinkering, I had no revenue goals in mind. I just wanted to break even, but more important, I wanted to create word of mouth. Money wasn't as important as growth—growth of my name and growth of my events.

Marketing folks rarely think these considerations are important in a world mired in analytics, attribution, and revenue, yet they're relevant to any startup—and even to the big players who run the risk of falling out of favor because legacy names mean little to new audiences.

TINKERING AND THE VALUE OF
INDIRECT INFLUENCES

There was one nugget I didn't tell you about. In 1992, there was no way to forecast how many people would come to your event; all you could do was hope. Hope, however, is not a strategy. There's an episode of *Beverly Hills 90210* in which one of the characters calls an 800 number to attend a secret party. (Remember that I mentioned earlier how M. Night Shyamalan was influenced by a Nickelodeon TV show when he wrote *The Sixth Sense?* The same is true of marketing, by which I mean you should never shut yourself off from anything because you never know what might inspire your next creative idea or help you find a way to measure impact.)

Today the 800 numbers provide event details. But there is something else that those numbers could give you: the total number of people who called and hung up. A close friend, Jeff Boyle, and I created a rough algorithm. We noted that for every seven calls we got, one person would show up to an event. So, if we received seven hundred calls, we were going to get one hundred people. It wasn't an exact science, but it was pretty close. The point is that our tinkering got us to use data that others had ignored and we unlocked new opportunities; in this case, we could track our marketing effectiveness.

Other DJs in the late 2000s used what they had learned from similar tinkering, along with new technology to create a worldwide movement. The scene they built became the most powerful, still active youth culture on the planet. Electronic dance music (EDM) is now mainstream popular culture that has spread throughout the world. And it's all rooted in the modern art of DJing, initially created by tinkering.

> **Geoffrey Colon**
> @djgeoffe
>
>
>
> Mass movements begin somewhere in small circles. Always pay attention to the fringes in order to find the future. #disruptivefm
>
> 7:23 PM—21 Feb 2016

Tinkering has helped build and market some unique businesses on the web. One example is a social-platform-meets-blogging-network-meets-creative-suite called Tumblr.

CASE IN POINT
The Tinkerer Who Built Tumblr

My wife introduced me to Tumblr in 2007. Allison had wanted to start a blog, but she found Tumblr was better suited for what she wanted to do visually. The design and functionality quickly piqued my curiosity. Today, Allison and I have three Tumblrs. Our earliest, allisonandgeoffrey.tumblr.com, was one of the first ten thousand blogs created on the site. As of 2015, Tumblr has 243.3 million blogs.

When Tumblr was launched in 2007, its creator was a high school dropout and New York native named David Karp. In 2012, I hosted Karp not once, but twice at Ogilvy & Mather for a discussion of how marketers were using Tumblr; we did this because Tumblr was uniquely different from other platforms. On my second day of work at Microsoft, Tumblr was sold to Yahoo! for $1.1 billion in an all-cash deal.

Karp loves his creation, and loves discussing how he went about tinkering to create and program its new functionalities. In his discussion at Ogilvy & Mather, Karp explained how tinkering continues to help build new features for Tumblr, and how tinkering by Tumblr users gives him ideas for ways he may not have initially considered to improve those products. "It's really one of the most rewarding jobs I can imagine," he said in a hushed tone, and then continued:

> I just can't begin to tell you how incredible a feeling it is to spend all day coding up a feature. I'm an engineer by background so I used to be involved in this product unit that was involved in building this stuff. How inspiring it is to spend all day building something that you have a hunch would be cool to use. And all you can really think through is maybe the way you could . . . use this particular feature . . . the way you would lay out photos, the way you create this particular post or this type of blog if you had this engine to customize themes and make them look any way you wanted. You can think through all the ways you would use it. You can kind of imagine your idols, the people you aspire to be like, or the creators that you admire [and] you can kind of imagine the ways they might use it. You have all these fantasies. You spend all day building this feature. Then you put it out there to the world and then you go home and the next day you come in and are completely surprised or often completely overwhelmed by all the ways these millions of people showed you how to use this thing that you just built. It is unbelievably rewarding, fulfilling; it's what gets us out of bed early every day. It's the greatest job in the world.

Karp understands that the creative class using his tools are the same people who will tinker in new and unique ways to influence what he may build next. Tumblr doesn't need a lot of marketers. Its feedback loop with users gives the company enough information to build new products.

The social network has changed how we interact and relate to content, and how that content informs our opinions of the world. It's changed how we learn, as well. Karp connects with customers who use the tools he makes in ways he couldn't have imagined. Instead of trying to control the scenario and forcing users to employ the tools the way he devised them, Karp pushes the customer experience out to additional customers. In some ways, his marketing is based on actual behavior in an organic setting. It goes against the knowledge transfer basics we marketing people were taught, which leads us to ask: "Are linear marketing experiences really the best way for customers to learn and ultimately adopt products and ideas?"

EDUCATION'S INFLUENCE ON LINEAR THINKING

Until about the age of twelve, we are rewarded in school with passing grades if we are able to recall information presented on multiple-choice tests—the same kind of tests that many students and their parents are now rebelling against because they don't measure the brain's lateral abilities or even begin to predict future success.

Susan Engel, professor of psychology at Williams College, wrote about curiosity in children and how it may affect them when they become adults and work in fields like marketing:

> The research in my lab shows that far from nurturing curiosity, schools seem to repress it. The pressures to deliver information, hone skills, stick to the plan, and avoid the unknown work against a child's natural curiosity. However, it needn't be so. Classrooms could be greenhouses for curiosity. Questions could be encouraged and guided, exploration could be at the center of the curriculum, and rather than being pushed to the side, children's specific interests could be fostered. Given how central curiosity is to learning and to human progress, why not cultivate it?

When we enter our teen years, we tend to put a lot of emphasis on what others think of us. We look for "social proof," also known as "informational social influence," a phenomenon whereby we adopt the actions of others in an attempt to reflect appropriate behavior in a certain situation. This sways our actions because we crave receiving "likes" from those around us as reinforcement of our ideas. The downside of this phase is that it constrains us; it makes us cautious about accepting new ideas and presenting our ideas to others.

By the time many of us begin our first jobs, the traits of social proof are so ingrained that we risk becoming averse to breaking through these boundaries. Instead of exploring new disruptive ideas, we get stuck continually asking two questions:

- Are people going to laugh at me for such a thought, message, or experience?
- Are people going to get angry or disagree with me for such a thought, message, or experience?

NONLINEAR THINKING'S IMPACT ON DISRUPTIVE MARKETING

Disruptive marketers seek to validate learning by getting people to laugh at their messages or to disagree with them. This approach is corroborated by research showing that people share things that make them laugh or make them angry.

While companies don't generally like controversial people or controversial points of view in their ranks, they will function at higher levels when they hire disruptive marketers to encourage the two types of messaging—humor and controversy—that receive the most customer feedback.

Geoffrey Colon
@djgeoffe

Data-driven marketers are weaker than marketers who possess both data and creative skills. #disruptivefm

2:48 AM—29 Feb 2016

The hiring practices of many marketing organizations push in the opposite direction; they exclusively recruit analytical minds. In a CMO.com study, Kimberly A. Whitler, professor at the University of Virginia, dissected chief marketing officers who were either very analytical, very creative, or both. Whitler found that

> CMOs with both analytical and creative skills are more likely to work in firms with stronger marketing capability. Balanced CMOs—that is, those with both right- and left-brain training—are more likely to work in firms with better marketing capability than either analytically trained or creatively trained CMOs. This speaks to the importance of being able to analyze and use insight to change consumer beliefs and behavior.

The study also concluded:

> CMOs with primarily an analytical background are more likely to work in firms with weaker marketing performance. This is likely surprising to many CMOs and CEOs, but it shows that only having an ability to analyze is not enough. Converting insight into strategies, plans and actions that impact the customer is equally important and requires skill. This is a cautionary tale to CMOs, CEOs and executive recruiters to not overweight analytical skills at the expense of creative skills.

While many think products with zero emotion or artistry can be built and grow to achieve mass adoption, we know that such products will never be accepted by a mass audience. The CMO.com study confirms this. Imagine the iPhone as a square, clunky metal box with BlackBerry-like keys. It would have no allure. What if the PayPal site had only text, no images? What if a Tesla vehicle were shaped like a big steel box? Would you use it just for its battery power? Doubtful, if another creatively designed product was to come along and make you feel more human and valuable.

Disruptive marketers are one-brain, 360-degree, holistic thinkers with multidimensional possibilities. We have the ability to create art *and* crunch data. To learn mathematical algorithms *and* write beautiful stories; to create action *and* visual appeal from unorganized sets of data.

This is the attitude and these are the skills you need to adapt to the changing world. It's a simple question: How do you meld diverse areas of thinking that have in the past operated independently? How do you synergize subject-matter areas into something brand new, like the DJs who fused two records in that early '90s midtown Manhattan club?

Geoffrey Colon
@djgeoffe

How do you create experiences that make everyone your marketer? That's what you need to answer.
#disruptivefm

7:26 PM—21 Feb 2016

Disruptive marketing is truly a blend of tinkering, psychology, sociology, anthropology, neuroscience, art, design, math, lateral thinking, predictive analytics, APIs, and measurement. It is not enough for a marketer to be all analytical or all creative—to be a search engine marketer or a graphic designer, to be a photographer or a coder. The marketer should be all of those things, and more. Viewing the world in silos is a linear, rational, and totally conventional way to approach marketing. And life.

So, how do we break with convention? One way is to flip convention on its head by creating and fostering an environment where everyone is or becomes a marketer.

THE END OF THE MARKETING DEPARTMENT

David Packard, cofounder of Hewlett Packard, said, "Marketing is too important to be left to the marketing department." He was right. Have you ever been a temporary worker? Better yet: What if you became a temporary worker in the next year? What would you do? What would you specialize in? What skills would you need to learn?

If you work for an agency, you're always a temporary worker. You keep your job as long as you retain business. Come to think of it, aren't we all temporary workers, since we all depend on selling goods or services in an uncertain economy?

For many years, marketers usually held full-time positions in organizations where they could live happily ever after—as long as they made no mistakes. Even in books about growth hacking, the hacker is the lone full-time marketing employee at a startup. Many marketing professionals who write books usually assume that all readers are permanent workers.

This isn't one of those books. In fact, I believe that having too many people too close to the product and the projects hurts marketing at many companies. That's because many permanent marketers can't escape their innate bias; they get too close to the product.

Geoffrey Colon
@djgeoffe

In the near future, orgs with people not rooted in bias by being close to the product will be the norm.
#disruptivefm

2:39 AM — 29 Feb 2016

In the agency world, most employees are treated as temporary. In this way, employees stay on top of their game with out-of-the-box ideas. This is essential in an economy based on creativity and imagination.

Granted, many vibrant economies, such as that of the United States, depend on permanent workers who receive generous benefits packages that include health care and retirement plans. Even though disruptive marketing is best when generalist professionals are temporary, our current pro-austerity system doesn't provide well for that. Nevertheless, the temporary generalist model works best for a disruptive marketing organization.

Contrary to what some believe, companies hiring temporary or contingent workers isn't a new model that arose out of corporate cost-cutting in the wake of the 2008 Great Recession. The practice of using independent contractors has roots that go back centuries. Indeed, there was a time when all workers were essentially "contingent workers," who hired themselves out to employers to perform a job or a service for a matter of hours, weeks, or even years, depending on the scale of the project. This changed with the industrial revolution, when manufacturers needed workers with specialized skills and so they increasingly began to hire full-time employees to work exclusively for their companies.

The assembly line was the main impetus for growth in permanent workers. Businesses ran on the economics of supply and demand, which included the labor pool. When the United States emerged from World War II with a surplus of labor and great demand for consumer products, there was a swing toward the corporate model, with knowledge workers as prized employees. Pushbacks in more recent years, with subsequent economics shifts and increased outsourcing, have reduced the ranks of permanent workers with cognitive knowledge, and now companies that want the best ideas need to bring in outsiders.

Not every company needs disruptive marketers, but when and if one does, having an old-style marketing department that is filled with entrenched specialists unwilling to execute new ideas won't help it reach that goal. The flexibility of temporary marketers is an advantage to these companies.

The Advantages of Temporary Marketers

Temporary marketing professionals, unlike full-time marketing executives, can easily bring the "marketing is not a department" philosophy to the organization. I first read about this philosophy in the 2010 book *Rework*, by Jason Fried and David Heinemeier Hansson. If you haven't read this book, buy, borrow, or steal a copy today and read it. It will teach you a lot about what work—and especially disruptive marketing—will look and feel like as the twenty-first century moves along.

Some of the lessons for disruptive marketers are:

- **Everyone is now a "marketer."** With the advent of communication platforms, no one team owns marketing anymore. In fact, the best companies realize that their customers now own the marketing outright. Employees simply measure the customers' pulse and design engagements to help prevent word-of-mouth churn and stalled feedback loops.
- **Marketing is a 24/7, 365-day activity.** Of course, you don't stay awake forever, like a robot. Software as a service (SaaS) and insights as a service (IaaS) are the disruptive marketer's friends. With tools like these, there's no need to hire lots of specialists.
- **Every time someone uses your product, it's marketing.** The tech world often forgets this principle. "Oh, we'll fix that next week." If so, then it's bye-bye ten thousand customers. If you can't build or maintain a good product, don't build one at all.
- **No amount of marketing will save poor products.** As I learned working in the music industry, "you can't polish a turd."
- **Customer identification surveys and polls that measure brand value are vanity metrics.** You're only as good as the next time a customer uses your product and tells their social media connections about it. No amount of brand marketing will help in this area. Brand marketing is a linear practice that made sense when communications were one-way and your value proposition was scarce. Now, products and services are in abundance.

Five Major Shifts That Changed Marketing Departments

In the past five years, there have been five large developments that have impacted the way we think about a marketing department.

1. **The enormous increase in available data.** Forget having no budget. Data is everywhere as long as you know how to access it. A search on Bing, Google, Yahoo!, Twitter, and Facebook,

as well as a plethora of other channels gives you varied information about what is going on in the world and what people are discussing. If you dig deeper, and have the budget, there are many tools to help you pull together various metrics to build predictive marketing models. I use a number of them, from Cision to Traackr, but have looked at other platforms, including Spredfast, Sprinklr, Hootsuite, Sprout, and Little Bird. Ten years ago, none of these tools existed. And we're continuing to see access to data increase even as the cost plummets.

2. **The increased access to mobile platforms with API integration.** Facebook, Twitter, Tumblr, LinkedIn, Pinterest, Snapchat, Instagram, and other platforms provide unprecedented access to billions of users, which not only helps you acquire new customers but also helps you activate, retain, and educate them over time. The number of these platforms is accelerating, and so are the ways companies can integrate with them to effect growth.

3. **The larger scale and greater speed of technology.** Today companies can reach a billion customers on a variety of interconnected devices. With this ability comes higher expectations about your company's and your product's growth. Conventional tactics, however, are too slow. Take a class on deploying APIs before you take any class on advertising and/or branding. When people in your organization ask about an API's ROI, tell them that determining ROI for an API is still something people are trying to figure out (just like ROI in social, digital, and other channels).

Measuring ROI on an API is not a simple calculation; it requires that you consider everything from the pricing of the API, which in many cases will be free, to how it could impact your business strategy. APIs are deployed for different reasons, including the ability to partner with other companies, to extract customer data, to enter new markets, to reduce the time of on-boarding new sellers, to collaborate more effectively with partners, and to establish a new business model. ROI for APIs is not a one-size-fits-all calculation.

Geoffrey Colon

@djgeoffe

A class on deploying APIs is more valuable than a class on advertising and branding. #disruptivefm

7:27 PM—21 Feb 2016

4. **The merger of technology and marketing.** Tools like Optimizely, Hubspot, Kissmetrics, and Marketo have made things that were previously hard a lot easier. Pilots that used to take weeks with web analytics can now be deployed in hours. But to make the full use of these tools you still need some solid technical knowledge. That is why the disruptive marketer is part IT, part artist, and part visionary.

5. **The rise of emotional intelligence as a required skill.** This factor is one with the largest impact, although the term is still fairly new. Created by John D. Mayer, of the University of New Hampshire, and Peter Salovey, of Yale, *emotional intelligence* (EI) has come to be defined as "the ability to accurately perceive your own and others' emotions; to understand the signals that emotions send about relationships; and to manage your own and others' emotions."

Jennifer Moss studies work culture. She is cofounder and chief marketing officer for Plasticity, a Toronto-based software-as-a-service company that helps organizations tool up their culture with happy and high-performing individuals. She is also the 2014 Stevie Awards' International Female Entrepreneur of the Year. Clearly, Moss is no stranger to the emotional toils of business. Moss believes culture is the most powerful marketing tool that many businesses have failed to embrace:

The best places to work have the most significant work cultures. People don't see this. It's a very subconscious feeling. Malcolm Gladwell talks about this in his book *Blink*; we can sniff out authenticity. I 100 percent believe that culture is the new marketing. Airbnb has customer experience and chief of people roles. When employees are in a thriving work culture, customer engagement increases; however, when employees are unhappy, their customer service decreases.

During my talk with Moss, questions about culture ultimately led to another trait important to disruptive marketers: EI. "We're going back to the old way of doing things," Moss said when I asked if the skill is important to marketing.

> High emotional intelligence by marketers is extremely important. In this new information age, machines and tech took over for hard skills. Emotional intelligence represents a desired soft skill that will drive technology creation and development based on the needs of people. Marketers will ultimately have to drive this because they are the voice for people.

While centering on EI and who has a better handle on those traits, I asked Moss a question that some may find controversial: "Do women—often shut out from leadership roles at companies—have better emotional intelligence skills than men? And, if that is the case, will they be better marketing leaders in the future?"

Moss doesn't believe one gender has better EI skills than another, but she gives women the upper hand when it comes to being more emotionally expressive—something that definitely is better for team building, bonding, and the ability to sense how customers are feeling, based on their body language or tone of voice. However, these skills are all learnable.

Geoffrey Colon
@djgeoffe

Although emotional intelligence is learnable, females are more expressive, which is highly valuable in business #disruptivefm

2:43 AM — 3 Mar 2016

Moss added, "Your DNA decides your personality traits but happiness traits like empathy and hope . . . are both highly malleable traits." I then asked Moss if businesses are taking EI skill building seriously.

"You have these superemotionally intelligent people burning to lead. We're going to see the same thing here with EI. Those organizations that fail to identify it as essential may be in trouble." According to Moss, companies with cultures that foster a people-first attitude will best withstand the disintegration of the marketing department. "Advertising will still exist," she said,

> . . . [b]ut [the] true leadership in companies [comes from] C-Suite execs who understand what resonates with people both inside and outside the company. . . . Your employees are your foot soldiers. The internal champions must become external champions. You start seeing companies with open accounting books and transparency. It will be people who are your marketers without a marketing title that will be the most valuable.

PART III

THE BUILDING BLOCKS OF DISRUPTIVE MARKETING

CHAPTER 7
CONTENT IS KING—
BUT DISTRIBUTION IS QUEEN

The speed of communications is wondrous to behold.
It is also true that speed can multiply the distribution of information
that we know to be untrue.

—EDWARD R. MURROW, American broadcast journalist

IAN SCHAFER IS the founder and CEO of a unique agency called Deep Focus, located in New York City. I've known him for some time, and we regularly tweet each other. In 2011, between my stints at 360i and Ogilvy, I interviewed for a position at his agency. Ian penned a piece on *Medium* entitled "WTF Is Social Media Anyway?" that gets to the heart of why so many conventional marketers have lost their way in the social world: thinking only in terms of content production. Schafer wrote:

Platforms like Facebook, Pinterest, Twitter, and Snapchat have eclipsed most traditional publishers as the power players in today's media landscape. More modern publishers (BuzzFeed, Mic, Popsugar, Vice) realize that the secret to their success lies not in time spent on their properties but the frequency of visits to their properties and the reach of their content, and how well they can monetize both. In fact, some of today's biggest media companies aren't the biggest because they own content (many don't), but because they do the best job at distribution. As opposed to publishers like Condé Nast, or portals/networks like Yahoo! who held top spots since the dawn of the digital age, platforms are best-suited to the current environment because they shift to consumer demands and are optimized for consumer context. They are tailored to the qualities of every consumer, each and every visit. Everybody's Facebook feed or Twitter timeline is different and uniquely theirs.

When people talk about "content marketing" or "native advertising," the "platformification" of media is the reason, and adoption of more social media and migration to mobile devices is the root cause. Content marketing has to exist because the platformification of modern media has behaviorally changed the people that we try to reach every day. They have become the sum of their personal and popular cultures more than ever before, as platforms become the places they not only express themselves, but discover their content. Thanks to platforms, people are increasingly able to live beyond the reach of advertising, with those very platforms limiting the amount of advertising people actually see, especially on mobile devices. That puts the pressure on us to evolve beyond just placing ads within people's social media feeds.

Schafer echoed a familiar refrain: advertising is no longer a page in a disruptive marketer's playbook, which raises the question: "Is content for the sake of content even the right approach?"

Geoffrey Colon
@djgeoffe

If content is king, distribution is queen and we know how powerful the queen is in the game of chess.
#disruptivefm

7:29 PM—21 Feb 2016

CONTENT CREATION AND THE NEW
DELIVERY SYSTEM

The social web and app ecosystem has been our distribution network for the past several years. Soon, the Internet of Things will allow content to reach various other devices, from your bathroom mirror to your car. To maximize their reach, companies are creating content to fuel this expanding universe. But will it work? Once most of us push "publish" or "upload," then we move on, looking for the next piece of content to produce results. Mostly, we don't investigate—beyond vanity metrics such as likes, shares, and views—whether that content is resonating with customers.

Enter *distribution science.* Several publishers already employ an analyst whose sole focus is to study how content will be shared. BuzzFeed is probably the most notorious. Its publisher, Dao Nguyen, isn't an expert in content creation; her expertise is in data science and content distribution.

I have always wanted to get to the heart of distribution science and prove to marketers that emphasizing content first and the creative process second is backward. However, to discuss this and similar questions on this emerging topic, I went to the Mecca of distribution science to learn how best to approach this new skill. On a hot and humid August afternoon, I took to the busy sidewalks of Manhattan's Flatiron District to reach BuzzFeed's offices in the historic Toy Building. I had scheduled a noon meeting with the vice president of business development and communications, Ashley McCollum. She's one of the brightest rising stars in the field of communications, so there was no one better with whom to discuss the role of distribution science, particularly how content and creative are now engineered.

Walking into the BuzzFeed offices on the day of the Windows 10 release, I entered a loft the size of a football field, full of MacBook Pros; there wasn't one Android or Windows phone to be seen. I couldn't help but notice also that I was probably the oldest person on the floor. McCollum greeted me with a huge smile, and asked if I was hungry as we joined a line for one of the company's chef-catered complimentary lunches. For a moment, I was transported back to the West Coast, and especially to a Silicon Valley tech company. The culture is very inviting. Everyone says hello and appears to be happy to be there. Who wouldn't want to be in a company valued at $850 million?

Everyone reading this almost certainly has interacted with something created and distributed by BuzzFeed on a social platform. BuzzFeed's growth, McCollum explained to me, has been anything but conventional. "Over the last three years, we've done zero paid advertising, zero acquisition programs, and no one has been singularly responsible for brand marketing. Everyone here represents the brand and marketing."

Geoffrey Colon
@djgeoffe

Ignore classic marketing strategy if you ever really want to grow fast. #disruptivefm

7:37 PM—21 Feb 2016

McCollum recalled that in 2012, when she arrived at BuzzFeed, she did the opposite of what her previous employer, NBC News, had expected of her:

> Often PR and marketing become so fascinated with classically trained strategy. As a result, you don't grow as fast. My goal here was to ignore classic strategy.
>
> We saw that social was this massive force in 2007, very early on; it was before social really was a thing. You could see how our homepage design changed as a result of social. [BuzzFeed founder] Jonah [Peretti] built a company around social. Most news was built at the time around search and homepage portals. We then asked ourselves how do we make the site better [to prepare for the coming reality of] social being the main distributor of content?

McCollum said that the people at BuzzFeed are data scientists at heart, who build content around the user experience of technology and devices. "We had a BlackBerry-optimized mobile website before the iPhone even existed." McCollum noted that every piece of content, every type of share button and API, is tested to determine how people engage with BuzzFeed content and where they distribute that content on their social graph.

> If you come to Buzzfeed from Pinterest, we've done tests [that show] there's only a 7 percent chance you tweet out that story. So why have a Twitter button on those pages? It makes more sense to play to where the user's actions will occur. So we increased the [number of] Pinterest buttons and usage increased ten times in terms of shares of content to Pinterest from that segment.

McCollum was also quick to point out that BuzzFeed helped tip the trend of many sites when it added WhatsApp share buttons to its content.

> We were the first site to do a WhatsApp button. . . . We noticed—again in tests on content—that many people were using that button to share content to the messaging app. It gave us validation into user experience. Shortly after that test and [after we added] the button to more and more of our site, other media websites followed and embedded a WhatsApp button.

In terms of creativity and content, McCollum and BuzzFeed are doing the opposite of what many marketers are taught: create first, distribute second. Instead, BuzzFeed seems to invert that approach: formulate where the content will be shared, then create the content to enhance the customer's experience. In this sense, they are one of the first customer-centric media companies in existence. McCollum opened her laptop and showed me a slide that explains the company's distribution philosophy. It looked like what is shown in Figure 7-1.

Figure 7-1: BuzzFeed Marketing Feedback Loop

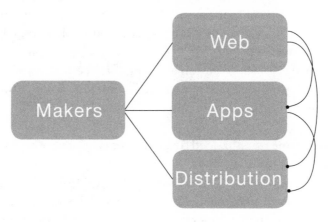

The first thing I noticed was that the word *content* doesn't appear anywhere. We do see the word *distribution* and can infer how it plays its role with the makers of content. The general lack of thinking about distribution science has made content marketing roles ineffective. Many are hungry to create and "publish," but most don't want to (or don't know how to) analyze those learnings and apply them to future cases. BuzzFeed seems to have empowered its staff with a content distribution-centric philosophy.

Although the goal of content is to capture customer mind share or persuade an individual toward action by creating contextually relevant experiences, good content never rises to the top on its own. BuzzFeed seems to understand this very well. But so do some other players.

CASE IN POINT
Building the Essential Playlist

Maybe the process by which I wrote this book, or how the music platform Spotify distributes music playlists (full disclosure: Spotify was a client of mine in 2011), will provide insight here.

Spotify approaches the art of building playlists with distribution-science acumen. Playlists are a huge part of their service; playlists are how many users find new content. And discovering content is by far one of the most difficult things to do in an overloaded world. So, building the essential playlist has become both a human and an analytical process. The data then informs Spotify what they should build more of and what they should abandon. It's different from the way a record label's Artists & Repertoire (A&R) person would do it, however. In the old days, they would sign an artist and then try to push that artist's career, even if it meant wasting millions of dollars.

Spotify uses a small editorial team to create the playlists, and as soon as an editor publishes a playlist, the listener data begins to generate feedback. The staff can then change and update the playlist based on the songs people enjoy, the songs they save, the songs they skip, and the songs that make them abandon the playlist. When editors see that people love the songs on tracks twelve or fifteen, they can immediately move them to positions one and two.

The Spotify team has published just about every shape and size of music playlist, providing every kind of music for every mood and situation. They have thought a lot about distribution based on the user's mood. But it's highly unlikely that marketers trying to push cloud services to potential buyers think this way when they're going to market with a content strategy.

Ex-Googler Shiva Rajaraman is the person behind the Spotify playlist distribution plan. Rajaraman understands that people don't build mega libraries of music around artists the way they did when iTunes was launched. Instead, they build playlists, which are rooted in the DJ mixtape culture. These playlists are inspired by key moments in people's lives—what they are feeling at a particular time. So the best way, Rajaraman realized, to connect people with music is through the heart, not the head.

As a music aficionado, I recognized that the overwhelming issue with Spotify was that you had to know what music you were searching for. For instance, if I was in the mood to hear Steely Dan, I could search for that artist. But what if I wasn't in the mood for a particular artist or genre when I logged into Spotify? What if I had no idea which artists I wanted to listen to? Today, the playlist culture that pervades the service enables discovery based on one's mood.

THE "DISTRIBUTION-FIRST" EDGE

Spotify is now built around moments in people's lives—and that's where the entire web is slowly heading. This is an approach whereby distribution data is handier than content data alone. What is the user's location? What time of day is she on a certain platform? What actions does he perform on that platform, and when?

Spotify has redesigned the entire distribution platform, bringing music recommendations via playlists to the forefront of the listener experience. This is a push/pull experience that the best distribution scientists understand better with each passing day. People want to find content, but sometimes they stumble on something they like and listen to it or share it; the experience feels serendipitous—but, in fact, it was designed with that intent in mind. It was designed to be at a given place, at a given moment.

Good content alone can't do this, of course. Distribution is the yin to content's yang. That's why more and more companies are trying to be the go-to resource when the time comes for specifics. Spotify wants to be that go-to resource when a person needs to listen to something. This "distribution is queen" attitude pervades other apps and services, as well.

CASE IN POINT
Find the Words, Create the Content

When I think of marketing resources, I am reminded of something called "Think with Google." Google realized that knowing how to use a product wasn't enough, so it created a tool to help advertisers gain the insights they needed to be effective. Through search engine marketing, Google Adwords helps customers using Google to find stores, services, and solutions via a wide array of direct and indirect education sources, among them practitioners, videos, and blog posts. It's what advertisers do strategically with the Adwords product as the world and customer behavior changes around them, however, that makes them effective.

The Think with Google education content hub was set up as a resource to inspire a niche audience of advertisers to take actions via strategic education and guidance. By creating a destination content hub, Google's product marketing team can direct traffic from the content resources they've created to specific product features provided by their business to track feature usage or adoption. For example, if Google is giving guidance on how to use "call extensions" (a feature that places a phone number in search results so customers can click to call) they explain the most strategic ways to utilize that feature. Click to call, for example, is used heavily by physical retailers who are trying to drive physical customer traffic and allows the retailer to track the phone calls that result in store visits. From Think with Google's thought leadership efforts, Google creates customers that invest and reinvest in their services.

Calling the Content Bluff: Why Distribution Is Essential

When I think of note-taking apps, I think of OneNote. You may be thinking of Evernote. The point is that there are only a few of these tools, and those that have succeeded have thought about distribution *prior* to creating content or a product.

Meerkat is a real-time video app that Twitter followers can view live. Of course, Meerkat was built on the back of the Twitter API so as to be discovered by the wide audience of Twitter users. Zynga became Facebook's go-to games solution because it had the best distribution. Catch my drift here?

A content guru will tell you that content is all you need to be successful in marketing. Disruptive marketers will call that bluff and explain how every successful entity became that way via distribution.

CONTENT CREATION AND PRODUCERISM

I've had the pleasure of working with many intelligent people. One of the brightest is Nicole Steinbok, senior program manager at Microsoft, where she worked on the OneNote product and now is involved with Surface devices. Steinbok was one of the creatives who, in 2014, helped launch the unconventional OneNote videos on Mac.

In a recent conversation about where marketing is headed, Steinbok and I touched on the topic of production. In an email thread, Steinbok added:

Marketing is going to be fully integrated in content we consume. At least I hope so. I hate ads. I cancelled Hulu because there are ads. I would pay more not to have ads interrupt my content, and I am not the only one. "Menutainment" is a term I saw at a Microsoft café. It reminds me of Benihana, where the chef cooks your food in front of you. Creating . . . food is also entertainment. I want to . . . see advertising/marketing itself be more entertaining or just completely integrated in[to] what I consume. I am sure others would detest [this] idea . . . because you feel even more manipulated. But I am fully aware that marketing/messaging manipulates me, I might as well enjoy it.

The main advance that I would predict with R&D is [that we will continue] to shorten the time window between R&D and the time it takes to go from idea to product to users' hands. I also . . . really enjoy being involved with Kickstarter. I am a customer, but I also feel involved with the development of the products I back through the updates I receive from the creators. I like that. I want more of that.

Making stuff is becoming easier and easier and requires less . . . scale. However I buy a lot of things, I don't have time or the motivation to make almost all of those things. But for people who are motivated to make stuff, so many hurdles are being removed or lowered. If I can contribute to making something by providing money up front (Kickstarter) or ideas or feedback I can see customers "making" more. . . . There are these machines in some of the Microsoft cafés where you can "make" your own type of beverage[. The café] provides tons of choices—what base flavor, what added flavor . . .diet, lite, zero, regular, etc. So although the user didn't make the machine, they are [given] a method [that] enables a type of making.

Steinbok was talking about what disruptive marketers call *producerism,* or the ability of anyone to create anything as long as he or she has the creativity and willingness to do so.

Lower Barriers Equal Ease of Entry

Producing things, Nicole Steinbok said, is becoming easier owing to lower barriers to entry. Chris Anderson touched on this in his 2006 book, *The Long Tail*:

> The traditional line between producers and consumers has blurred. Consumers are also producers. Some create from scratch; others modify the works of others, literally or figuratively remixing it. In the blog world, we talk about the "former audience"—readers who have shifted from passive consumers to active producers, commenting and blogging right back at the mainstream media. Others contribute to the process nothing more than their Internet-amplified word of mouth, doing what was once the work of radio DJs, music magazine reviewers, and marketers.

Some people have dubbed this the "Architecture of Participation." Figure 7-2 shows how it works.

Figure 7-2: The Architecture of Participation

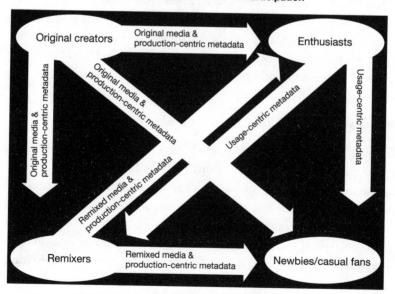

This model is one of the reasons podcasting is now so massive.

CASE IN POINT
When the Walls Came Tumbling Down

From 1990 until 1996, I produced a weekly radio show called "Furthur" on 91.3 WLVR-FM in Bethlehem, Pennsylvania. I loved it. Every week for four hours, I played tunes from around the globe for a small audience of around two hundred listeners. This was at a time when the producerist tools lay in the hands of big companies who could afford the technology.

Fast-forward to 2006. While working for a startup in New York City, I discovered a company out of San Francisco, called Podsafe Music Network. It was a podcast hosting and discovery network before podcasts were mainstreamed on iTunes. Podsafe hosted and promoted hundreds of podcasts that were similar to the radio shows I had produced in the 1990s. At the time, however, the tools needed to produce a podcast were not simple—there was a high barrier to entry.

I loved listening to some of those early podcasts, but I didn't have all the technology required to get back into the broadcast booth. Then in 2012, a startup called Spreaker emerged, which allowed anyone to use its tools and technology to create and distribute podcasts. So I did what anyone who loves broadcasting would do: I began recording a podcast called "Disruptive FM." Spreaker gave me (and millions of others) the creation tools. As a result, podcasting—a form of producerist culture—is exploding.

Universal Access: Now Anyone Can Be a Producer

In 2014, Edison Research found that 39 million Americans had listened to a podcast in the previous month. That's a decent number of listeners, but consumption isn't the whole story. Based on a scan of podcast directories, it appears that on any given day a person can access an average of fifteen thousand shows.

In the past, if you or I didn't have access to media-creation tools, we couldn't take action. We couldn't produce anything. We simply had to consume the content that the outlets pushed on us. But that situation has changed in the past decade. By 2020, it will tip even further.

None of this "producing" requires professional equipment anymore. Just like the rise of self-publishing and video creation, audio creation is now universally available. With an iPhone and apps like iPadio and Spreaker, my four-year-old can produce a podcast. As Chris Anderson so eloquently forecasted over a decade ago, none of us is simply a consumer anymore. We are also the producers.

THE IMPACT OF PRODUCERISM ON DISRUPTIVE MARKETING

If we are producers, we can also be marketers. Disruptive marketers understand this and use it to their advantage. For instance, what if I could influence a few of those creators to advocate on my behalf, based on whatever it is they are interested in?

Today, productivity technology exists in many shapes and sizes. There are no barriers to entry as there were when only a small percentage of people owned the tools of manufacturing and creation. Now, individuals have the same access to those tools. This new era of widespread productivity can be a pitfall, though, for particular brands and the legacy companies. Corporate-created content, goods, or services aren't enough anymore. The ability of anyone to create is the new manufacturing and marketing world. Creation, no longer confined to the few, is now open to us all.

I spoke to Anthony De Rosa, former editor at Circa and Reuters, now with *The Daily Show*, about how news startups are cropping up daily using producerism as their marketing vehicle.

Merely existing and not having to lean on big capital to survive is in itself a disruptive form of marketing. De Rosa thinks because you don't need to produce things en masse but can find a target audience, it is leading to an explosion of niche news sites.

"Traffic right now seems limitless on the web. If you're starting out now, if your focus is niche, you do things small and do things at a certain scale, you can do some really innovative things in news media. You can find an audience and that audience can help spread the word. Covering a subject of interest from a niche angle becomes your marketing."

De Rosa thinks that in every part of media, sites that focus on niche are driving the producerism aesthetic.

There are a lot of really great examples of small and niche projects within media right now that can succeed. The Marshall Project is a perfect example. They've found a topic, the criminal justice system, and they can own that topic. So if anything does come up in the news around this subject . . . , they're the center point. Because they're niche focused they'll grab attention on that topic if and when it becomes front and center within the context of larger news. It's hard to go after and build some things without serious venture capital, but if you can be seen as an expert in an area and produce and host your own content, you can do well when the audience distributes that news for you.

Geoffrey Colon
@djgeoffe

Everyone can produce any content now. Brand content looks mediocre to some UGC content now. #disruptivefm

7:58 PM—21 Feb 2016

What Comes Next: Producerist Trends

In addition to niche content sites, we will see some additional trends as a result of producerism:

- Product experiences for customers that crop up in a matter of days, not months, owing to cloud computing
- Short-form videos and commercials produced by people, not professionals or agencies
- Fashion design from people in their bedroom "studios" that is replicated via 3D printing and spread throughout the world, with zero need for a Fashion Week or for mainstream press coverage

- New food-sourcing opportunities that tap into desires for natural ingredients, not chemicals
- Broadcasts created and distributed by anyone who has something creative to showcase
- Self-published books that incorporate embedded Vines, Instagrams, or Snapchats
- The first mobile social network that goes beyond "sharing" and gives people the tools for "creating"
- Ability to access the president of the United States' State of the Union address on Medium

Instagram, one of the fastest-growing social networks, is more than a distribution platform. It is also a creative platform.

What Disruptive Marketers Create

What if I told you *everything*? Seems like a pretty broad objective, right? However, what if I told you *nothing*? You might feel differently about that.

In a brave new world where the customer base will do the creating for a marketer, with your inspiration as their guide, why do you have to create anything at all? Well, you still need to inspire people to produce that content for you, based on the brand's authenticity. Here's how you do that: stop thinking about platforms and forms of content—images, videos, etc.—and start thinking about human behavior.

As I noted earlier, in 2012, IBM tasked my team at Ogilvy & Mather with creating a plan that would illustrate how people "share." In essence, we learned instead why the most disruptive marketing attempts produce inspiration and create emotional resonance. Disruptive marketers don't create content and they don't produce viral videos. They strike the match that gets everyone else to ignite. (Our findings were eventually reported in a white paper, "The Science of Sharing," which was based on research done by the *New York Times*.)

This is why every year, platforms like YouTube see more than three hundred remixes of songs that were not commissioned by the artist or the artist's label. It isn't YouTube that's inspiring this behavior. It's that those up-and-coming laptop producers want to be famous themselves. They realize that producing original music, while it is important for any creative person to do, isn't going to get them discovered by "influencers." They believe it's better if they remix a song by a major artist—even if doing so means breaking copyright law.

HOW TO BE A PRODUCERIST

Customers have changed. Audiences are now more likely also to be producers. They want to have complete control over what they see and share. Think about the last video you searched for and watched on a platform like YouTube. Who produced it? Did it look professional? If so, did it look as if it was made to live for only a short time? Do you think the producers understood that they had limited time to spend on that piece before they would create and distribute their next conversation piece?

Focus on Platforms, Not PowerPoint

The best way to be a marketing producerist, then, is to ditch the PowerPoint and create your strategy live, on digital platforms, in real time. Doing everything on a platform lets you learn the user experience right away and gives you agility. It also allows you to feel the dynamic experience of how customers behave on that platform. That is, a traditional PowerPoint strategy is 2D and linear. Yet, the way people act and behave, how they share and retweet, and the extent to which they engage and produce UGC (user-generated content) isn't in any way flat. Explaining a web strategy using PowerPoint is like trying to explain 3D using a regular pair of glasses.

Platforms are your canvas, your wilderness. You leave a digital trail that allows you to see what works and what doesn't, and lets you adapt to the changes on that platform that occur on a weekly basis.

At one time, Facebook was the place to build a community. In 2009, I spent too much agency time trying to persuade companies that they should build a community on Facebook. But those slides are more "tell" than "show." The best way to demonstrate how a platform works is to get on it. That's a much more immersive step than a PowerPoint deck. As Frank Rose noted earlier, marketers want to use a conspiratorial whisper, not only with our customer audience but also with the clients, partners, and coworkers we are trying to convince should adopt a disruptive marketing approach.

Today, if someone was to ask me what to do on Facebook, I would open up Facebook ads and show them all the rich data targeting they can use to reach audiences. Facebook has pivoted from a social community to an ads network, but no amount of PowerPoint slides will show this better than simply logging in and experiencing the service itself. There's a reason visual education is increasingly popular; it resonates in ways that text knowledge transfer does not.

Learn from the Early Adopters: Hire Young People

I had the good fortune of having great mentors. I now understand why they hired me when I was in my twenties and kept me on their teams. I enjoyed telling them what was coming next in the industry. This is an important marketing function, because it allows companies to pivot their brand strategy before their consumers do—so the brand stays at the top of their minds and relevant wherever they go. The best way for a firm to stay relevant is to hire young people; young people like to find the future via a combination of search, social data, and netnography (the study of human behavior on the Internet). This is especially a role most suited to a young data punk.

The other reason firms want young people is that young people pay attention to trends, and that helps you determine where the producerism is taking place, who is doing the creating, and what they are using to do so. In 2006, while in the agency world, my interns told me to ditch MySpace for Facebook; and in 2011, they told me to adopt Instagram. None of this would have happened if I didn't have younger team members to mentor me.

How the world has changed. As a result of technology, mentorship needs to be inverted. Traditionally, a marketer wanted a seasoned veteran as mentor. But a veteran may be bogged down in the day-to-day—too busy managing to create things—whereas it is unlikely that young people are managing a team; they have more time to be enthusiastically inefficient. For this reason alone, seek them out for your team. Along with their other skills, they can add value to your emerging media marketing plans.

During a visit to a startup office in San Francisco in 2015, I noticed some young data punks (ages twenty-two to twenty-five) spending the majority of their time working on their smartphones. In the near future, it's highly unlikely that many of us will be producing user-generated content on a MacBook Pro, or even using Windows 10. More likely, the primary tools of future generations will be smartphone apps (and some of those apps might not be created exclusively in a digital ecosystem;(I'll touch on the post-digital movement in chapter 8).

Young adults on the social web are much like young followers of pop culture. They are early adopters, they are participatory, they enjoy creating and not simply observing, and whatever they adopt will probably be used by all of us in due time. Ignore the "snake people" articles you've read and hire one now.

CHAPTER 8

SOCIAL BY DESIGN
AND THE ADVENT OF THE
POST-DIGITAL AGE

I grew up in a physical world, and I speak English. The next
generation is growing up in a digital world, and they speak social.

—ANGELA AHRENDTS, Apple senior vice president

- "Why does your website have so many social pieces of content embedded in it?"
- "Why aren't you following corporate protocol and using our template?"
- "We want to push as many people as possible to our property, not that of others."
- "What do you mean you used a content strategy strictly on Snapchat? We need blog hits!"

SPEAK SOCIAL: THE NEW WAY TO CONNECT

These are common utterances from marketing people who don't get it. They fail to understand that a traditional, controlled strategy in brand marketing moves too slowly today, that it involves way too much process, and that it has too little impact, unless you are dealing in investor relations and the strict SEC rules that apply there.

Today's customers want to be able to engage with content and share it across the many places they inhabit. Trying to control the audience flow is like trying to control customer journeys. Customers are people. People can act irrationally. If you understand and accept this, you can connect with them on their terms, not on yours.

Social by design is a design strategy that encourages and facilitates conversation into an ongoing relationship-management model. Instead of onetime, interruptive messages from someone who behaves like a used car salesman, social by design by a solutions provider armed with emotional resonance is a real conversation using content, creativity, and product information that's presented from a customer-centric point of view. In these social-by-design conversations, marketers express who we are at the same time as we learn and get feedback from our customers about how to make our products—or, better yet, the world—more inspiring.

Geoffrey Colon
@djgeoffe

Social by design is a strategy that puts people ahead of commerce. #disruptivefm

8:03 PM—21 Feb 2016

Socially designed products put people and the culture of companies—not data, devices, customer segments, or information—at the center of the user experience. It's a fundamental shift in the way the web and its platforms are structured. Most likely, social by design will come to define the next phase of the social web, in which we are all makers, producers, and participants.

Instead of technology, devices, or products being the selling point (as it is with operating systems like Windows 10, Android, and iOS, or applications like Word, Keynote, and Photoshop, or devices like iPhone, Galaxy, and Lumia), conversation is the selling point—the interaction with other people centering on emotional triggers. The data collected from these conversations, mostly concerning how these items fit into our everyday lives, helps encourage further product improvement and innovation.

Ongoing conversation (not just customer feedback loops once or twice a year) between you and those who use your products or who inhabit your industry space is the only true way to know what people are and are not looking for.

But let's get real. Although social by design sounds good in theory, brands are terrible at practicing it. Cindy Alvarez, author of *Lean Customer Development* and director of user experience at Yammer, agrees. In one of our several informative back-and-forth email chats, Alvarez talked about how brands still don't understand the role that social by design plays; many still employ one-way tactics that are only beneficial to their needs, not to their customers' needs. As Alvarez added:

> When my facial scrub is cheerfully saying, "Follow me on Twitter," I just cringe. Come on, technology. We can and should learn from the offline world. People have transactional relationships and social relationships and it's not that hard to differentiate them. . . . Social relationships aren't necessarily "better." Just ask someone who has grown unhappy with their hairdresser or mechanic, but can't bring themselves to "break up" with that service provider. So what makes people want to "listen" to a brand? Sounding like a human, ugh; that's table stakes. If that's all you can say about your social approach, you're not trying hard enough.
>
> I also don't think it's about product quality. There are products I love and actively recommend, but don't want a social relationship with: Blendtec, for example, or Trader Joe's, Crazy Egg, Starwood.
>
> There are two types of brands that I see really succeeding in building that relationship these days. I'd call them identity brands and improver brands.
>
> Identity brands align with how we want to live and how we want others to see us. Think of Nike, and "Just Do It"—that feels like it's all about the customer and her identity. Contrast that with the big brands that have been suffering for years: "I'm loving it" and "Open happiness"—can you even remember which brands those represent? Possibly not, because they are embarrassingly generic.

Lifestyle brand?

Improver brands want to help us be smarter, faster, and more attractive. These brands speak more like a helpful human guide, offering suggestions, ideas, or recommendations. They don't operate on the level of big recognizable taglines; [instead they offer] tons of tiny little suggestions. Think of You-Tube stars—Michelle Phan or the You Suck at Photoshop guy, or companies with engaging, educational blogs like OkCupid or Kissmetrics.

What Alvarez was saying demonstrates that even a fundamentally new communications design approach isn't used very well by brands. As she noted, the best social-by-design experiences aren't built strictly within a social network ecosystem, yet many brands still confine themselves to such thinking.

Content Marketing: The Cornerstone of a Meaningful Brand

When it comes to discussing social by design, another good person to bounce ideas off of is Julian Mitchell, who creates social-by-design content for a living. He is a senior brand writer for BuzzFeed, working out of Los Angeles. Mitchell is no ordinary marketer. In fact, I don't think he would welcome the label. His main goal is to spark and advance conversations, elevating the way people think.

We call people like Julian "inspirers." They don't fit the Malcolm Gladwell description of "connectors, mavens and salesmen" described in his book *Tipping Point.* That book, first published in 2000, is dated now because of the social-by-design world. When asked how disruptive marketers can adopt a social-by-design philosophy, Mitchell's answer hit at the heart of the concept:

In today's digital climate, content marketing is the key to building a meaningful brand that really impacts people in a way that enlightens, provokes thought, shapes perspective, and ignites conversations to ultimately form real, lasting connections with people. You want to leave a powerful impression. Content marketing is the emphasis of every media plan marketers control, which is where most of the global ad dollars are being invested—content, conversations, and experiences. With that said, I think the key to effective disruptive marketing is creating compelling or provocative content, or experiences that generate content that sparks conversation. It's abrupt, authentic, unapologetic, and driven by a specific mission or intention. Great disruptive marketing introduces a disruptive point of view that forcefully challenges the status quo. . . .

I think technology plays a pivotal role in disruptive marketing efforts, but functions as the other half that enhances the content experiences. It serves as the tool, platform, or gateway. As a result, I don't think disruptive marketing is limited to technology. I think we've seen great examples with the Truth's brilliant, yet hard-hitting antismoking campaigns, or what Beats has accomplished with their emotionally arresting Hear What You Want campaigns that deliver captivating stories from a unique and untapped point of view that aligns with real time to inspire further dialogue. Brands like Red Bull have mastered disruptive marketing through the context of extreme sports with their remarkable stunts, such as skydiving from outer space. Taking a more tech-driven angle—what Jay Z did with Samsung, launching his album in tandem with their new smartphone, releasing a content series that gave people unprecedented access into the creative process, and having the brand buy one million copies so it went platinum prior to release—changed the RIAA rules for good. Tyler, The Creator's Cherry Bomb app, is a perfect example as well, launching out of nowhere—complete with a full album, merchandise, access, rewards, original content, and a space where fans could feel as if they owned a piece of real estate in their platform.

The Essential Component: Emotionally Intelligent Leaders

My conversation with Julian Mitchell quickly turned to a key point that was also made by Jennifer Moss earlier about company culture. That is, simply to execute a social-by-design strategy isn't enough to

bring success. Emotional intelligence in the culture of the leadership is also vital. As Mitchell noted:

> The brands that will win won't be the ones who seem like peers;
> they will be the brands that are our peers. I honestly think
> companies that will benefit most are ones that actively seek
> and acquire creators and curators, putting them in creative
> leadership positions to freely be who they are within the mis-
> sion of the company. They will be smart, savvy people who live
> in the culture the brand thrives to connect with—that speak
> the language, reflect the style, and embody the attitude of the
> intended audience. By nature, the marketing efforts and con-
> tent experiences will be organic, authentic, intriguing, and rel-
> evant; and [will] hit on those critical nuances. Anything else
> will be a manufactured version that falls short. Then, success
> will be dependent on research and studying things like neuro-
> science for these answers. Social media isn't the only channel,
> but social media is what makes the experience real and digest-
> ible for this generation.

Talking with Mitchell did exactly what social by design is supposed
to do. It sparked conversation that made me think. It asked myself
this difficult question: "Am I marketing for a company whose culture I believe in?"

How about you? If your answer is no, then are you doing what you
are doing simply because marketing is what you enjoy doing? Are
you marketing a product or set of products that you actually use?
What motivates you? The chances are that if you don't believe in the
culture of the company, you're going to have a hard time designing
experiences for the people you are trying to connect with on a creative level. In the future, that will become apparent to others—especially those you are trying your best to inspire.

Where Social by Design Is Headed

Julian Mitchell, quite the futurist when it comes to experiences, led
me to ponder the future of marketing, and how social by design

flies in the face of everything that conventional wisdom has taught me. Mitchell suggested:

> By 2025, television on your timeline will be real—short, epi-sodic programming that anyone can distribute directly to [his or her] followers. Studios, brands, and influencers alike will all have channels—on Snapchat, Periscope, etc. Social media will officially be social entertainment; dial-up curation [will] be the custom content experience. [At the same time,] users [will be given] real estate on the [social media] platforms they champion, so the communities [will organically] form without leaving the platform. Marketing will be a more free-form in-dustry run by creators, curators, and free-thinking visionaries who have completely [eliminated] corporate language to tell stories and introduce formats foreign to us now. It will be about truly customizing and curating your own experience in every moment, controlled directly from your mobile device.
>
> Video will transition into 3D and VR [virtual reality] experi-ences. We'll start to see VR as a staple at live music events, such as festivals and tours—allowing people to be digitally transported to stages and unlock other experiences. Everyone will have the quality to shoot award-winning content from their mobile de-vices. Because that will oversaturate the space, the transition will then move into live stream video—increasing in length and ex-posure. I can see people eventually moving into a space where they are comfortable keeping a live feed on themselves all day.

If Mitchell's predictions are correct, could our lives look like the one depicted in one of the most controversial documentaries ever created, *We Live in Public*? This film examined the idea of people trading in privacy for constant connection. The implications are im-mense. How does this view of the future reshape what we know as media? Will there be a need for gatekeepers anymore when every-thing can go direct?

If this is the world we are moving toward—forget about mar-keting, for a second—our entire world will be reframed, as will how we live in it.

THE NEXT WAVE: THE POST-DIGITAL AGE

We shall not cease from exploration
And the end of all our exploring
Will be to arrive where we started
And know the place for the first time.

—T. S. ELIOT,
Four Quartets,
presciently written in 1941

In 1998, MIT Media Lab cyber pundit Nicholas Negroponte pointed out in *Wired* magazine, "We are now in a digital age, to whatever degree our culture, infrastructure, and economy (in that order) allow us. But the really surprising changes will be elsewhere, in our lifestyle and how we collectively manage ourselves on this planet." Indeed, we've been through a lot as marketers in the last half century. We've gone from print to radio, to television, to Big Media, to the Internet, to social and mobile, and from physical worlds to virtual worlds. Now we are about to undergo what has been dubbed the "boomerang effect," by which we come full circle and reenter the physical and analog worlds in reaction to digital acceptance.

Exciting things will take place, thanks to the Internet of Things. In fact, in as few as ten years, 2016 marketing operations will have gone the way of the transistor radio. While conventional marketers slowly aim their marketing toys at the digital sandbox, disruptive marketers will be back to playing in the physical world!

Disruptive Marketing Comes Full Circle

It is important to understand that just as art imitates life, technology shapes both life and art. Many marketers who follow art trends are bound to see the technological world shaping our understanding of how we experience reality. Problem is, while the real world is digital now, disruptive marketers are already moving on to the "post-digital" space.

Geoffrey Colon
@djgeoffe

In a post-digital world, marketers use any and all tools,
not simply digital tools. #disruptivefm

8:05 PM — 21 Feb 2016

With electronic commerce now an accepted part of the business
fabric, the medium of digital technology in and of itself holds less
fascination for marketers. The term *post-digital* does not mean or
aim to explain life *after* digital; rather, it describes the opportunity
to explore how the digital age intersects with humanity.

Post-digital investigation is concerned with our rapidly evolving
relationships with digital technologies. It says that being human is
not just being digital. If you compare digital and post-digital, the
differentiating factor is the economy of reality. By this I mean that
it's people, not simply technology, who bind relationships—even in
a world overrun with technology.

In a post-digital world, disruptive marketers think of digital as one
medium in their cache of tools. You need the right tool for a particular job, and disruptive marketers don't go for the high-tech option
simply because it's available. Indeed, that digital option might not
be the best way to communicate with a desired audience. The latest
digital toys sometimes fail to impress, simply because people are not
all that interested.

This is the essence of the post-digital era. If we look at emerging
trends, surely they have a place for innovation, but they also deal
with human connections and the desire to embrace a better future
for the world. Marketers who understand this are more likely to take
actions that get customers to connect based on experiences and
education, rather than take actions designed just to get customers
to buy. Disruptive marketers are as interested in people as they are
in technology—probably more so than those who call themselves
"digital marketers."

Insights & psych

Leaders who align with this post-digital Zeitgeist can tap into the true feelings of humanity as it evolves into 2020 and beyond. But who are these post-digital leaders? They represent a cross section of the world—artists, customers, business owners, academics, technologists, bureaucrats, students, Millennials, Generation Zers, Generation Xers, Generation Yers, C-Suite executives, entrepreneurs, developers. Everyone.

PART IV

FOUR SKILLS
FOR THE
DISRUPTIVE
MARKETER

CHAPTER 9
SKILL #1:
ALWAYS BE LISTENING

No one wakes up excited to see more advertising, no one goes to
sleep thinking about the ads they'll see tomorrow.
—JAN KOUM, WhatsApp cofounder

HAVE YOU WATCHED one of the many video clips on YouTube that
show scenes from the classic film *Glengarry Glen Ross*, based on the
David Mamet play? One of my faves shows Alec Baldwin as Blake.
Blake is a real estate salesman sent by corporate goons to drum up
more business from the tired and whipped sales team. In one of the
film's most intense scenes, Blake castigates the team with this harsh,
unmotivating speech:

> You got leads, Mitch and Murray paid good money. Get their
> names to sell them. You can't close the leads you're given you
> can't close shit. You are shit. Hit the bricks pal and beat it be-
> cause you are going out.

The team complains that the leads are weak. Then, during a pro-
fanity-laced, pompous back-and-forth, Blake explains how sales and
marketing work, using a simple, second-grade analogy. Pointing at
a blackboard, he says, "ABC. A Always, B Be, C Closing. Always Be
Closing. AIDA. Attention, Interest. Decision. Action."
This is the core of classic interruptive marketing. Yet it rarely works.

INTERRUPTIVE MARKETING VS. DISRUPTIVE MARKETING

Interruptive marketing is dead. Just don't tell Ken Wheaton, managing editor of *Advertising Age*. Wheaton wrote a 2015 op-ed lashing out at disruptive marketers' dislike of interruption as a strategy:

> Media fragmentation is our reality. It's not going anywhere. I'd like to think that at some point it will stabilize. And it probably will. But sometimes it's hard to believe, especially when you read stories about time shifting, cord cutting and a generation of children who think they can just watch whatever they want whenever they want on that thing Mommy keeps in her purse.

Wheaton may be hostile to disruptive marketing because the industry he is in—publishing—is itself going through many changes. Wheaton continued:

> The funny thing is these disruptors have a big problem with interruption. That's the problem with traditional marketing. It has the gall to "interrupt" consumers' daily lives with lame things like TV commercials and print ads and direct mail. Left to these guys, we'd go from a rather polite "Pardon the interruption" aimed directly at a consumer, to talking about them behind their backs and saying things like, "We're gonna disrupt the hell out of them. Gonna scrape up all their data and stalk 'em around the web. They'll never even know they're being advertised to." One of the more damaging things the disruptors do is convince marketers that there's something almost shameful about old-school advertising and marketing methods. You can't interrupt. You have to attract.

Wheaton's suggestion that data and retargeting make marketing disruptive is wrong. His argument doesn't cut to the core, which is that as marketers we are ultimately trying to relate to people via culture. Relating to people requires social cognition. It requires a conversation about aspects of the world that go beyond mere selling or interrupting in an attempt to capture attention. It goes beyond profit-and-loss columns on an Excel spreadsheet. Wheaton noted in his op-ed that if companies want to market effectively, they must stimulate people to buy something. Yet while sales are always a barometer of success, disruptive marketers believe it no longer is the barometer of marketing.

Geoffrey Colon
@djgeoffe

There's a reason you have two ears and one mouth. Always be listening to what customers are saying. #disruptivefm

8:08 PM — 21 Feb 2016

Disruptive Marketing's New Criteria

Many disruptive marketers emphasize growth first, sales second, as I have mentioned earlier. Others emphasize conversation first, sales second. Putting this into the context of the conversation I had with Frank Rose, this means that marketers and salespeople must become disruptive, because it allows individual prospects to string together evidence and find the solution they are seeking. But what if customers don't string together to reach a solution a company likes? In disruptive marketing terms, that's not failure. It's more data pointing to what you can do to improve your services!

Advertising doesn't follow this approach because it doesn't speak to people. It yells at them. Wheaton's analysis of interruption is better left to an era in which "spray and pray" was the main strategy of the media-buying culture: First, you *spray* your message everywhere to interrupt an audience, and then you *pray* that the audience will buy your product.

Targeting audiences on the social networks and targeting intent by using search advertising have obliterated the need for "spray and pray." Disruptive marketers don't need to *reach* a mass audience because they don't need to *appeal* to a mass audience. We target our audiences with a microscope. We believe that the best way to gain your audience's attention for a relevant discussion is by inverting Blake's *Glengarry Glen Ross* model. That's ABL: A Always, B Be, L Listening. There's a reason our species evolved with two ears and one mouth.

Listening in the world of marketing is more powerful than speaking.

The Different Impacts of Talking vs. Listening

The ABL approach to closing a sale puts emphasis on listening rather than on talking. Data gives disruptive marketers the indicators of what people want, so the companies can go back and make, redesign, or enhance their products. Looking solely at the messaging is an antiquated view of marketing.

Susan Cain noted this powerful philosophy in her must-read book *Quiet: The Power of Introverts in a World That Can't Stop Talking.* Cain says what most conventional marketers seem to forget: that in the Western world, we have metamorphosed from a "culture of character" to a "culture of personality." In this new culture, impression—how someone thinks about you or how you are perceived—is more important than character. When applied to interruptive marketing and advertising, this performance indicator shows that by always talking, always being on, and always at hyper speed, marketers can force an audience to listen and then lead it to the buy.

My argument against that approach in our noisy world draws on Cain's study: we have an innate bias in our social world that leads us to believe talkers are better leaders, although the facts show otherwise. She reported in her book:

> We perceive talkers as smarter than quiet types—even though grade-point averages and SAT and intelligence test scores reveal this perception to be inaccurate. In one experiment in which two strangers met over the phone, those who spoke more were considered more intelligent, better looking, and more likable. We also see talkers as leaders. The more a person

talks, the more other group members direct their attention to him, which means that he becomes increasingly powerful as a meeting goes on. It also helps to speak fast; we rate quick talkers as more capable and appealing than slow talkers.

If Cain's view is correct, in the future the top brands will rarely speak; instead, their audience (their customers) will be the talkers and we marketers will be the listeners, making and building products based on loudly announced needs. Rebecca Carlson and Eric Drumm agreed that, based on Cain's data, the way companies use social listening is ineffective.

"How many times have we spent hours and hours pulling a listening report and then presented a sixty-page deck and the client goes, 'Thanks for putting this together,'" Drumm said, sounding discouraged. "Then in your next talk with them . . . when [you] ask if they [took action based on] any of the insights, they shake their heads no. Even though you have actionable insights in the listening report, nothing ever changes." In other words, brands just keep talking, fearing that if they stop, we will forget what they had to say.

Carlson thinks many companies don't even use the art of social listening:

> In terms of business insights, I would hope companies would use social listening to inform business decisions. I worked [for] a client [which] only targeted men in their messaging. We showed [them that] 30 percent of their audience was female and [that it] was likely that more women were buying their product for the household or had an interest in a particular area . . . the product inhabits. Data can disprove cultural inferences and innate biases, which is always a good thing.

Data, Emotional Intelligence, and Social Listening

There is still a big issue with social listening. Because of the technology, it isn't a definite science. "Even when people do take a hard look at social data, they take the human element out of it," said Drumm, adding:

Tools have a hard time reading sentiment or figuring out human culture. Yes, it is labor intensive but you can't just look at the numbers, you have to use your emotional intelligence to take the temperature of what's really happening and data analysts aren't that human. . . . Plus anybody can pay Sysomos a monthly fee and learn items about their query strain regarding their brands. When brands are thinking about data, they think that they have to pay IBM to use a Skynet server for $200 million. That's not true; data is cheap and it's only going to continue to get cheaper.

Geoffrey Colon
@djgeoffe

Customer behavior data is everywhere now. How do you use it? #disruptivefm

8:13 PM—21 Feb 2016

Data is in abundance and it is becoming cheaper to obtain via APIs. Yet, not a marketing conference goes by when I don't shake my head in disgust at least once. It usually occurs during the first day, in the first presentation following the keynote. The slide goes up and there in bold glory is a linear customer journey with buzzwords like *engagement, conversation,* and *amplification.* The presenter loudly proclaims why it's so important to engage with your audience, but I can't help feeling that even though they want to show connection with their customer, their approach is no different from the advertising shilled by conventional marketers.

These customer journeys, and the marketers who present them, tend to simplify the rationality of human beings when it comes to communication design, impulses, actions, reactions, and triggers. As noted by several behavioral economists, including Richard Thaler, author of *Misbehaving: The Making of Behavioral Economics,* it doesn't really work that way. No, duh.

Disruptive Marketers Advantage:
The Cognitive Whisper

One thing about conventional marketing that always falls short is lumping people into target segments and then pushing a button to publish content that the marketer assumes those folks will see. The conventional marketer doesn't understand the enormity of online activity. Figure 9-1 is a dramatic illustration of what typically happened online in just sixty seconds during the years 2012–2014. It increased exponentially in just those three years.

Figure 9-1: What Happened Online in Sixty Seconds, Years 2012–2014

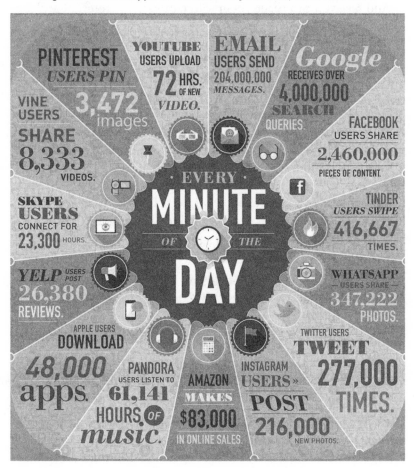

Because of all this activity, the disruptive marketer gains an advantage in using the cognitive whisper. Yes, you need to publish content and stories that reach your desired audience. But before you hit Send, what is the design of the story you're about to publish? If your attitude is, "This is what I want to tell the customer; this is the narrative we want to state; this is the message we want to CONTROL," well, consider the value of transparency, authenticity, and collaboration. These are the three traits customers want from brands; they do not want to feel they are being preached to.

ABL (Always Be Listening) captures customers' moods. You can find out what they're seeking. You can pinpoint the problems they cannot find solutions to.

And *then* you can reach them with contextually relevant and personal content.

HOW THE ABL APPROACH WORKS

Are you using the ABL approach? Let me show you how it really works.

I ran listening reports on the types of businesses and organizations that were asking questions about transitioning their marketing. The organizations identified included:

- **Fortune 500s**—Businesses trying to transition from a legacy model to a modern marketing model using Big Data for more real-time audience engagement.
- **Midsize businesses**—Companies trying to figure out what marketing techniques and strategies to adapt to their fast-growing, yet—from a historical perspective—young organizations.
- **Startups**—Businesses trying to figure out which marketing tactics will be the most effective for them. They may not have much in the way of budget or resources, but they do have enough organic growth that they must move rapidly from inbound to outbound marketing.

Here are the job titles of those asking these questions:

- **Fortune 500s**—Marketing managers, marketing directors, CMOs

- **Midsize businesses**—Marketing directors, search advertising managers, content strategists
- **Startups**—Growth hackers

Next, I found data concerning what those individuals liked in terms of content within the larger social web:

- Content marketing
- Big Data
- Social media
- Podcasting
- Video
- Corporate storytelling
- Art
- Culture

- Technology
- Sports
- Retail
- Travel
- Finance
- Women's issues
- Volunteering

I created a list of news sites that this audience followed on Twitter:

- Bloomberg
- Bloomberg West
- *Harvard Biz Review*
- *LinkedIn Pulse*
- *Fast Company*
- *New York Times Tech*
- *BBC Tech*
- *HuffPost Tech*
- *BuzzFeed*
- *CNBC*

- *Marketwatch*
- *Vice News*
- *Mashable*
- *TechCrunch*
- *Fortune*
- *Marketplace*
- *Forbes*
- *Recode*
- *The Verge*

With this data (and a lot more) came creative ways to pitch new stories. For example, there is little need to use an ABC (Always Be Closing) model that shouts "Advertising!" if what you are selling isn't what people are seeking as demonstrated by their actions (based on social data). There are alternative angles and approaches that don't deal with marketing per se, that are still attractive (art, culture, technology, etc.) and could be used more effectively.

In the future, with the ABL (Always Be Listening) model, disruptive marketers don't need to do real-time marketing to be effective. I know, you may be scratching your head because you keep reading that real-time marketing is the freight train to which you need to hitch your locomotive. But that train left the station years ago. In fact, the warning is: Don't do it! Marketing is moving into an on-demand world. As a disruptive marketer, you need to be prepared for it.

ON-DEMAND MARKETING

Digital marketing is about to enter a new territory, one that will be a lot like Netflix binge watching. When you find a film series you want to watch, you opt in and watch the entire series, beginning to end. Thanks to the consumer power that's been brought on by mobile devices, marketing is headed in the same on-demand direction—and it's not just always on or always real time. It's more contextually relevant and responsive to an individual's opt-in for marketing experiences that cut through the clutter with micro targeted precision.

Helping usher in this on-demand scenario are search technologies like Bing, along with mobile apps and the social web, which create an anything-at-any-time environment for users. This has made product information plentiful. Plus, it's more than marketing material that is pushing this on-demand behavior. When you book a flight on Expedia, it's productivity and convenience, not a marketing action. Other sectors of the digital world, just like other business models in industries beyond marketing, are major influencers of what experiences people expect from these organizations.

And this is just the beginning. Before us lies a landscape of mobile growth and the Internet of Things, of connected devices and productivity applications like Cortana, Google Now, and Facebook's Moneypenny. We are moving into a world where searching in a box will feel antiquated as we perform searches by voice, gestures, and images. In fact, searching may become a whole new world of UGC, as some engines allow photos to be uploaded into large pools available for public use (think Shutterstock meets Flickr meets Wiki). The iOS interface already allows instant image sharing between handsets via the cloud, as well as the ability to pay for purchases with a thumbprint.

But the biggest development that will transform marketing is wearables. We have yet to see its power in marketing, but we are transitioning to a point where products like Apple Watch will change people's experiences—and ultimately affect marketing. Instead of a website that sells clothing by featuring photos of the product, people will be able to try on the product virtually to see how those jeans look before they use a right swipe to share that image with friends and obtain their feedback. Only then, with enough high ratings, will they move into purchase mode.

Over the next several years, we're likely to see the consumer experience radically integrated across both physical and virtual environments. One technology that's gaining traction is near field communication (NFC)—embedded chips in phones permitting exchange of data on contact with NFC-tagged objects. Beacon technology will know when you enter a particular store; then based on your browser history, the NFC technology in your phone will display items that are in your size and color preference.

Indeed, immersion will come into play in the world of on-demand marketing in ways that you may never have imagined.

CASE IN POINT
The Circle Is Unbroken

Here's a customer scenario that is only five years away from being mainstream:

Scene 1: Olive sees a friend and admires her Marc Jacobs handbag. She taps her iPhone against the headphones because both devices contain NFC.

Scene 2: Olive's phone prompts her to photograph her torso; next, it displays how that same handbag would look on her shoulder and in various colors. Olive can even switch the color of her top so she can figure out how the handbag goes with different outfits.

Scene 3: Olive shares those photos with friends on Facebook using an application called BevyUp and polls them on whether they like or don't like the handbag.

Scene 4: Meanwhile, a notification pops up on her phone from Amazon Fashion telling Olive if she purchases the handbag from ⌄

Amazon and signs up for a Prime account—she isn't yet a member of Amazon Prime—she will save 20 percent. Olive signs up with one-touch verification that syncs her Amex account directly to her Amazon registration via an API.

Scene 5: Olive's friends like the handbag in brown and Olive completes the purchase.

Scene 6: When the handbag arrives the next day from Amazon Prime, Amazon asks her if she wants to post an "unboxing" photo of the handbag to Instagram with the #AmazonUnboxed for an additional 10 percent off her next purchase.

Scene 7: When Olive meets with those friends who voted in her handbag poll, the NFC chip in the handbag signals her phone, which reminds her of a 20 percent off first purchase for those who register for Amazon Prime.

Scene 8: Every week Olive gets a notification about the events going on at Foundation, a Seattle nightclub that she regularly attends. Foundation has an integrated relationship with Amazon Fashion, which tells Olive that if she carries the handbag to the club and posts photos with the tag #FoundationFridays, she will be granted VIP access for a month. A board at the entry outfitted with NFC and beacon technology welcomes her by name upon arrival.

Scene 9: At the club, Marc Jacobs pings Olive's phone with a Spotify playlist that's contextually relevant to her tastes.

Scene 10: The next time Olive is in Nordstrom, her phone gets a notification that she should stop by the café for a complimentary beverage, courtesy of MarcJacobs.com. She obliges and enjoys a cold lemonade on a hot summer day.

These scenes from Olive's life illustrate the on-demand world that disruptive marketers need to be building and programming right now. Many of its features tap into human behaviors that have been created by a mobile on-demand world:

- Customer urgency
- Customer immediacy
- Customer contact
- Customer personalization
- Customer simplicity

- Customer interaction (to help shape data footprints and improve productivity)
- Data integration (for better decision making)

These also tap into content, such as music, that we don't often think of when it comes to consumer engagement. One of the few universal-branding languages, music is hardly ever used by many brands unless they have licensed it for a television advertisement. But disruptive marketers realize that different modes of content can act as forms of currency to build "feelings" with their audiences. To win over those on-demand customers, you must know them, including what they expect and what works with them. Then, you need the ability to reach them with the right kind of interaction. Data lies at the heart of efforts to build that understanding—data to define and contextualize trends, to measure the effectiveness of activities and investments at key points in the consumer decision journey, and to understand how and why individuals move along those journeys.

But don't get all worked up over Big Data as your savior. Remember that data represents the actions of *people*, and people still have to put that data into action. Thus, we have the need for disruptive marketers to shape the bright, shiny world of Big Data into what makes it truly powerful: insights.

CHAPTER 10
SKILL #2:

DON'T BE LURED BY BRIGHT, SHINY OBJECTS

A company shouldn't get addicted to being shiny,
because shiny doesn't last.

—JEFF BEZOS, founder, Amazon.com

Big Data is the hot new buzz term. You hear it everywhere in the marketing world. There is nothing intrinsically wrong with Big Data; the problem is not how much data is available, it's how it is used.

CASE IN POINT
Ask the Right Question

The night I was introduced by a mutual friend to my future wife, Allison, at a Manhattan nightclub, I asked her what she enjoyed doing. Not what she *did*, but what she *enjoyed* doing. The information I was trying to elicit was different from what I would have learned had I asked what she did.

My question gets to the root of what truly drives people. Work is only part of life; it isn't life itself. We tend to forget this if we define ourselves by what we do for a living, rather than what we do to live. And just because a person does something for a living at a certain point in time, that doesn't mean she will do it forever. Things change constantly.

THE PROBLEM WITH BIG DATA

Understanding what drives people lets you tap into their emotions, which in turn lets you know whether or not you will connect with them. Many conventional marketers don't ask those questions. They assume they already have the answers in the Big Data that comes in their market research.

Marketers and advertisers chase the big shiny object because it makes them appear relevant. Yet in their quest for relevance, they forget that the goal is to achieve an ongoing customer relationship, not a momentary trophy. That's why I asked my future wife what she *liked* doing. Jobs come and go. If you choose a person based on a job title, where does that leave you when that job no longer exists? A better reason to choose to be with someone long term is that person's character, which remains regardless of job title. The same is true of all our other connections.

That objective is sometimes difficult to achieve in a world in which it often seems power is ceded to the extroverts who chase the shiny trophies. Instead, we should be following the introverts—the quiet creatives and data philosophers who understand how to turn insights into action.

I tried a little experiment while writing this (that's what automation allows), and found that the term *Big Data* was mentioned on social media 955,578 times between April 1 and July 1, 2015.

That's only three months! If that rate holds, in one year the number of references to the term will reach around 3 million—and that's just on social media. Add the other analog and digital sources where it might appear and the number probably increases three or four times.

THE VALUE OF BIG DATA

Steve Goldner is an avid blogger on the topic of social media. Residing in my old stomping ground of Maplewood and South Orange, New Jersey, Goldner goes by the alias "Social Steve" on both Twitter and his Wordpress blog. He is one of the most outspoken critics on the subject of marketing talent in this transformational era.

"I think the biggest issue that we have in the world of marketing right now and possibly why we're seeing a lift in disruptive marketing is because it's creatively tied to data," says Goldner. "A lot of younger marketers can't relate marketing to executive KPIs [key performance indicators]. Then you have a lot of the older marketers who haven't stayed up on the new trends and tactics. This is not a skill many people have. I bet the majority of them will be reading this book." Even the term *Big Data* puts the emphasis on data collection as the bright, shiny object. Big Data sometimes emphasizes the wrong things, though. For example, the emphasis on collection for collection's sake is misguided. The emphasis from a marketing perspective should really be on data-driven insights or a new term just starting to crop up in marketing circles, *Insights-as-a-Service* (IAAS).

Capgemini, a French consulting technology corporation, defines IAAS as deriving value from data. And isn't that the point of collecting it in the first place? Yet, the goal in the world of Big Data shouldn't be to collect data. That's an action. The goal is to use the data to derive strategic insights from its analysis.

Most conventional marketers have gotten stuck on the act of collecting Big Data, when what they really need are the insights within these mountains of data. Tanner Christensen, product designer at Facebook and author of *The Creativity Challenge: Design, Experiment, Test, Innovate, Build, Create, Inspire, and Unleash Your Genius*, thinks Big Data causes us to forget about what and who is within those mountains.

People are far more interesting and complex than a set of data, but really aren't we all just bits of data anyway? The difference, I think, is in how we frame the pursuit of that data and what it means. Information that we pull from a database can be immensely helpful for design or creativity—in that it can help us identify trends, spot outliers, and make informed decisions. However, information we associate with *behavior* and *intent* is vastly more impactful. Precisely because it gives us a better way of interpreting the data.

Looking at data strictly from a "data" perspective is limiting. Add on the reasons the data exists in the first place, the influences on it, etc. and you've got something you can actually influence and learn from. Mining data from a database is great for shining general trends or insights, but unless you get down into the reasoning for what caused that data to begin with, "Was someone having a bad day? Are there cultural trends at play? Was something misleading or confusing? What were the *intents* behind the data?" you'll be blind to much of what influences your work.

THE END OF MARKETING AS USUAL

If we remove the shiny Big Data label, we are left with conventional marketing and conformist tactics. And if we are rebelling against this thinking, then we are also rebelling against HIPPOs. No, not the animal, but the acronym for Highly Paid Personal Opinions. We know based on design learning that the person with the highest salary or biggest title doesn't necessarily make the best business decisions—especially since tenure means little and everyone has access to an abundance of data at his or her fingertips.

HIPPOs may also be the reason big, shiny, sparkly things exist in the business world in the first place. If your bonus is tied to these metrics, then you're going to move the business toward achieving them, even if they have little impact on business. The C-suite and high-level executives may dislike me for saying this, but you won't make progress unless you foster debate.

I write and speak a lot about data-driven decisions mixed with creative solutions, and I think there is no single best way to do it. If you make *only* data-driven decisions, you'll lack creative execution. And if you make *only* creative decisions, you're ignoring the data you need to measure the impact of your strategy to determine if it's working. To me, the perfect business world is one in which smart creatives are 50/50 analytical/creative hybrid thinkers. Data is a flashlight; creativity is a key used to unlock opportunities. This goes for all industries, from engineering to medicine, film production to education, and everything in between.

The Future of Data in Decision Making

So, how will data be used in the future to reassess the decision-making hierarchy? I spent much of August 2015 in Brooklyn, New York, working on this book. As part of my research, I met with many old acquaintances who are working in a variety of industries. I wanted to ask them who the decision makers are in their fields. One question I asked each of them was, "Is there a strict work hierarchy or do you have an agile meritocracy where you work?" If they answered "a hierarchy," I followed up with, "Does this hierarchy hinder really unleashing the power of marketing in a customer-focused manner?"

More than half of those I asked responded with something like, "Geoff, the situation is terrible. There are a bunch of people with big titles, bigger salaries, and corner offices telling everyone what to do based solely on their opinion or gut-level feelings." The idea of customer focus at their workplace was simply given lip service.

Clearly, this isn't the case everywhere, but of the twenty people I asked, more than half answered this way. In such cases, the hierarchical structure of organization charts—status quo reporting and layered job roles—prevents disruptive ideas from ever finding a place to be tested. The good news for disruptive marketers (and the bad news for those clinging to conventional organization charts) is that we won't be living in this world much longer.

Tech companies like Amazon, Facebook, Microsoft, and a slew of startups are dismantling their organization charts. Very soon, data will determine how great an impact a person makes at work. It will also help people make quick pivots to correct real-time missteps. When this changeover happens, many will rejoice, because they can ride the wave of adjusting solutions based not on conjecture, bias, or defined roles, but on data. People all over the world are rejecting defined roles when it comes to gender, race, and class, so why should we bind ourselves to outmoded definitions of how we do our work? HIPPOs and the hierarchical model may actually be hurting companies. While I don't mean this as an attack on experience, I do agree with the statement (of uncertain origin, but often assigned to W. Edwards Deming) that "without data you're just another person with an opinion." Data scares the opinionated conventional marketing managers. Their approach to making strategic decisions is an "I know a good marketing plan when I see it" strategy. Why? "Because I have twenty years of experience knowing when a marketing plan is good!"

Any job requires a mix of skills, from thinking to collaborating, to creating, to doing. In the future, more and more of the doing will be done by software rather than by people. There's nothing wrong with this; in our creative economy, automation will free up more time for us to do other things. What many seem to miss when they chase those bright, shiny objects are the essentials of good marketing: collaborating with others, formulating ideas, and bringing those ideas to fruition.

The Coming Shape of Marketing

A very opinionated colleague at Microsoft loves to discuss the field of marketing. He is good at balancing the yin and yang—of teaming the most radical in the field (including me) with the most conservative (names withheld to protect the innocent). Matthew Woodget is a senior product marketer and storyteller for Microsoft Business Solutions. At one time he was an engineer.

Matthew is the best example of an outsider looking in and reshaping marketing. Matthew and I get into conversations—usually over a beer at the Microsoft campus pub—that, if it's a sunny summer day in Seattle, can sometimes go on forever. His views are informative on the subject of chasing bright, shiny objects versus looking for a harmonious balance, and for recalibrating objectives by constantly identifying opportunities through Big Data:

> As with all things in life, balance is key. No doubt technology has and will continue to enhance how marketing is targeted and delivered. The content, however, will continue to require the human touch; that is, unless you plan on having your marketing target robots. . . . Until that day comes, humans will need to experience a sense of connection and purpose with the companies that they interact with.
>
> Something that all the machine learning and artificial intelligence in the world can't do yet is [tell stories]. The ability to synthesize a multitude of concepts, generate new ideas [and]

metaphors, and predict how others feel (what neuroscientists call "theory of mind") are all uniquely human qualities. It is through these and other capabilities . . . that we are able to create . . . content that connects with other humans. . . . How we reach those humans personally *and* at scale (call it "Personal at Scale") is where the magic happens. It is [also] where we can rely on algorithms and the *rock star data scientists* to reach the right people in an agile, nimble way.

Matthew paused, and added, "As with many industries, much of the skill set eventually gets automated and we are pushed further and further to the realms of the idea economy. [However,] the uniquely human quality of creativity . . . will be commoditized last, if ever."

Geoffrey Colon
@djgeoffe

You can't commoditize creativity, at least not yet.
#disruptivefm

8:39 PM—21 Feb 2016

Story making is still a huge part of the skill set that cannot (at least not yet) be taken away from the human marketer. So, while many talking about disruption are going to continue to talk about Big Data as marketing's savior, creativity still reigns. Matthew finished his pint before getting to his final thought—the one that makes him one of the top marketers at Microsoft:

We must use all tools at our disposal. I often like to give direct mail [marketing] a hard time. Yet in some cases it still serves a purpose. If new technology teaches us anything, it's how to use the old technology in a relevant way. When new technology bursts onto the scene, it's always characterized as the solution to world hunger. Then reality sets in. This is a good thing. It means we end up using the right tools for the right job. And sometimes a phone call makes all the difference in an authentic relationship.

For someone to act on what we land with them we must engage with them. To engage with them we must be relevant. To be relevant we must be authentic, and share the authentic voice of our existing customers. Those things together unlock trust. It's a lack of respect [for] these *innately human qualities* that leads so many companies [astray], whether it is using Twitter as another dumb broadcast channel, spamming people with email, or robocalls. You can't automate trust.

THE MISSING LINK: QUALITY

Although Big Data helps us target customers using push methods, it's important to remember that bright, shiny objects usually lose their luster over time. You can have the greatest data in the world, but if you don't have a good product or a good company culture, you're going to have a hard time going forward.

Among the things you need to ensure longevity is the right people filling the marketing functions—people with the right DNA and the right cultural fit.

How to Find Quality People

You ask questions, just as I did of my wife on that night we met. You stop asking about skills. You stop asking about an Ivy League education. And you stop asking about job titles. Instead, you are inquisitive, you use your emotional intelligence, and you start asking prospective staff about what motivates them, what they enjoy doing.

The problem most organizations have with moving toward a disruptive marketing mindset is that their marketing departments comprise marketers who have:

- Advanced degrees, such as MBAs
- Economic, creative, or artistic backgrounds
- Traditional mindsets when looking for growth solutions

Such people:

- Make decisions based on guesswork and hierarchy.
- Create one-way, controlling communications aimed at awareness.
- Employ a tired value proposition to make prospective customers want to use the product, solution, or service.

Instead, organizations should seek, and you should try, to move toward:

- Data geeks with the souls of artists who have the business acumen of a Sheryl Sandberg and the storytelling skills of a Don Draper.
- Highly collaborative people who don't sit in a silo and can break down walls to be part of design-thinking, design-oriented teams.
- Analyzers of data who:
  - Build interactive experiences with the audience.
  - Possess a high emotional IQ and empathy.
  - Have walked in the shoes of others and, therefore, can help create solutions and products that people want to use, not market products people couldn't care less about.
- People who live the culture of the company by setting the culture of the company.
- People who don't wait for the CMO to give them direction and who don't like top-down hierarchies. They are part of the company's hive mind (collective consciousness).

Many companies are lucky enough to find these candidates; when they do, the battle is on to retain them.*

---

* Unfortunately, some of these candidates are unable to translate data into executive performance indicators, which should always be a requirement.

CHAPTER 11

SKILL #3:

GIVE BACK: ETHICS AS THE NEW MARKETING

> [A] world in which government is burdened by historic debt, philanthropy has limited resources, and the private sector is only interested in its own personal gain is simply unsustainable.
>
> —SIMON MAINWARING,
> branding consultant and blogger

IF YOU EVER attended an Occupy Wall Street demonstration, you may have heard this chant: "People over profit!" The flattening of the world economy and the advent of social communication media allow us to know how companies that manufacture our clothes, harvest our coffee beans, and assemble our smartphones treat their employees, care for the environment, and so on. The implications for marketing based on company behaviors are immense.

Buycott is a mobile app created by Ivan Pardo, a Los Angeles–based developer, that scans the bar code of any product in your grocery cart and traces the ownership of those goods all the way to the top corporate parent, including conglomerates like Koch Industries and Monsanto. Pardo explained that he made the app to empower consumers and their consciences. In a 2013 *Forbes* interview, he said, "I don't want to push any single point of view with the app. For me, it was critical to allow users to create campaigns because I don't think it's Buycott's role to tell people what to buy. We simply want to provide a platform that empowers consumers to make well-informed purchasing decisions."

The biggest transformation to business in the last fifty years hasn't been mobile computing or the influence of Millennials. It's a larger undercurrent that will pull down many businesses in the next five years. In fact, it may be the single most disruptive movement to affect marketing since the advent of the radio advertisement. Its name? Corporate social responsibility, or CSR.

MARKETING AND CORPORATE SOCIAL RESPONSIBILITY

You may have heard the term. You may have ignored it. Recently, I was talking with some marketers at a Brand Innovators event in Seattle. I asked ten of them this question: "If you have only $15,000 to spend, should you spend it on a message about a product's price point or on social media customer service?" Their answers may surprise you. The data showing how they should have answered will surprise you even more.

Geoffrey Colon
@djgeoffe

Marketers think customers are motivated solely by price. But 1 in 3 customers said they are motivated by customer service. #disruptivefm

2:52 AM — 29 Feb 2016

Nine out of ten responders in my unscientific poll noted that they would use that money to create more price point awareness. Only one said she would put the money into a social media customer service program. Is this because they think customer relationship management (CRM) is unsexy, quiet, and boring, and they misunderstand how powerful it can be with customers? Probably.

My colleague Lin Huang at Bing Ads recently studied how social signals affect brand reputation. His results confirm that more and more customers leave brands or service providers because of customer service issues. So, if you have a low-priced product and you aren't going to follow up by providing proper support, they are going to churn in droves.

Of course, many people in social media like to complain, but it's still a marketer's responsibility to handle those issues. Some might not think so, but customer service is as much a part of marketing now as is amplifying narratives. Customer service may also motivate existing customers more than another brand-perception campaign or television ad. In fact, many of the customers who put customer service at the top of their list and don't care about price *also* don't want the companies they do business with to be pillagers of the world's resources.

Geoffrey Colon
@djgeoffe

Are ethics the new marketing? #disruptivefm

9:24 PM—21 Feb 2016

To truly understand the impact that CSR has on modern-day organizations, consider that Millennials, who number 86 million in the United States, think social responsibility is an essential quality in the companies or service providers they do business with. Before they hit the Pay button, they want to know that the company gives back to society in some way.

While brands appealing to the baby boomer generation in the 1980s and Generation X in the early 2000s could simply profit from providing a service at a low price, Millennials are steering away from companies they perceive are solely rooted in profit. To test this theory I sometimes ask my Millennial friends to read this quote from Microsoft's former CEO, Steve Ballmer—and then I video their reactions:

We've grown from 18 percent of the profits of the top 25 companies in our industry to 23 percent of the profits of the top 25 companies in our industry over the last five years. Profits are up over 70 percent, where the industry profit is up about 35 percent. Pretty good.

That's pretty good if you are speaking to boomers, but Millennials don't want to hear about that, even if they are shareholders. They want to know what you are doing to advance the world.

Companies whose marketing is truly disruptive realize that you can't just be philanthropic and assume customers will buy your product or service. The way to keep customers interested is to have a culture that lives its belief in social issues and thinks beyond sales. Before you decide to ignore this observation, consider that seven out of ten Millennials regard themselves as social activists, according to a 2011 study by TBWA/Worldwide. You ignore this warning at your own peril if what you care about when it comes to marketing is a spreadsheet showing increased product adoption.

What doesn't look, feel, or sound like marketing now actually *is*. Some other data about Millennials' views to consider are the following:

- One in three will either boycott or support businesses based on the causes they care about. They tend to reward organizations and businesses for their involvement in social causes.
- Four in five say they are more likely to purchase from a company that supports a cause they care about (if price and quality are equal) and three in four think more highly of a company that supports a social cause.
- A stunning three in four believe that corporations should create economic value for society by addressing its needs.

Earlier I noted that if you are to adopt a disruptive marketing mindset, you can't simply think about business as usual. That last bullet point is why. If three out of four young adults believe companies need to create economic value for society, that translates to companies actually having to "give back."

Giving back comes in many shapes and sizes, but for the most part, it isn't about giving back in the form of dividends to shareholders.

For this reason, CSR has become a prime area of focus for disruptive marketers; it is often more important than many other initiatives. CSR is such a large part of business now that universities have entire departments dedicated to the practice. One is Boston College and its Center for Corporate Citizenship, part of the Carroll School of Management. I sat down with the school's director of marketing and communications, Tricia MacKenzie, who said:

> I think that companies are embracing CSR because they are seeing an actual impact in brand loyalty and revenue. At 86 million strong, Millennials are helping to drive this change. Research reports that 50 percent of Millennials make an effort to buy products from companies that support the causes they care about and they have a high expectation for companies to make a long-term public commitment to CSR. Companies are reacting to this by incorporating CSR as not simply a "nice to have" but an integral part of their long-term business strategy.

I asked MacKenzie to drill deeper, and discuss what falls under the CSR rubric. She elaborated:

> CSR goes beyond community giving. CSR is fostering an inclusive work environment, cutting net carbon emissions to zero, building transparency through a sustainable supply chain—companies are setting these goals and a notable list are actually achieving them. The question is, "What is your organization's vision for the future and how do you progress towards that vision?"

WHAT COMPANIES NEED TO DO TO BECOME SOCIALLY RESPONSIBLE

While CSR sounds impactful, the reason some companies don't bother with CSR and many conventional marketers brush it aside is that it can be difficult to push organizations to adopt what is essentially a lifestyle change. As MacKenzie told me:

After a company builds a strong definition of what success looks like by incorporating a CSR program they will not only need to change their policies in place for systems and products, but they will also need to change the expectations of the consumer. This will not be achieved by preaching about saving the world with buzzwords. Companies are going to have to build on a demonstrated commitment over the long term, dedicating communications and marketing resources to inform the consumer with data and reporting on these efforts. Word of mouth is challenging to measure. The data shows that companies who do well for the world do well in the long and short term. Therefore, CSR goes beyond word of mouth to a results-driven strategy which integrates the consumer via communication tactics.

If CSR integrates the customer in the company culture, I wondered whether this didn't force companies to be more open about how they operated. MacKenzie explained:

The currency of leadership is definitely transparency. The two-way medium that social media creates can reveal how a company invests in the environmental, social and governance dimensions of business. PR will no longer solely manage a company's reputation. The reputation of a business is not dependent on crisis management or product marketing; its reputation is built by transparency. Transparency with customers, stakeholders, partners, employees—these are the foundation of a CSR program. CSR is the platform and social media is the message delivery vehicle. Companies are actively facing communication challenges understanding the value of CSR across departments and adopting [it] into their overall brand messaging. A company with an engaged digital audience must treat that audience as active storytellers of the company's efforts to "do well by doing good." Therefore, companies that are the most transparent are leading in building a world in which we want to do business and a world in which we want to live.

But what, I asked, if you are a company that literally pollutes the earth or exploits its employees' labor? How do you adopt CSR as part of your overall marketing initiatives? Can you? MacKenzie noted that giving mere lip service to social responsibility doesn't work; it won't solve a company's problem because it isn't authentic:

> This is a challenge for most companies—it's a large conversation to choose a CSR initiative that is tied to your business purpose and makes sense strategically for the investment. However, many companies are setting stakes in the ground supported by marketing efforts, paving the way for others to do the same. There are many excellent examples today. One that stands out is CVS Caremark. CVS Caremark is the largest retail health company in the U.S., with 200,000 employees and 7,800 locations. By being the first national pharmacy chain to make the decision to stop selling cigarettes in 2014, they eliminated $2 billion in possible revenue yet, by promoting a tobacco-free lifestyle, the company aligned more strategically with their mission to improve the quality of health for their customers.

In other words, CSR must be a long-term, ingrained-in-the-culture-of-a-company strategy that flies in the face of PR crisis communications, short-term quarterly profit models, and Wall Street earnings calls. Disruptive indeed.

CHAPTER 12
SKILL #4:
LEARN, UNLEARN, RELEARN

You don't learn to walk by following rules.
You learn by doing, and by falling over.

—RICHARD BRANSON,
founder and CEO of Virgin Group

In my favorite book, *Future Shock,* author Alvin Toffler wrote: "The illiterate of the 21st century will not be those who cannot read and write, but those who cannot learn, unlearn, and relearn."

Geoffrey Colon
@djgeoffe

When was the last time you did something for the first time? #disruptivefm

2:52 AM—29 Feb 2016

Unfortunately, I've met many marketers who chastise others because they themselves lack the skills they need in this new world. So, instead of humbly admitting that they need to learn more, they undermine the people whose skills they don't understand.

The concept of the hive mind is powerful. I use it with every team I lead. Its manifesto in business is, *There is no smartest person in the room. The room is the smartest person in the room.* In other words, the collective is more powerful than any one individual.

MARKETING'S BATTLE WITH OBSOLESCENCE

Education experts estimate that up to 40 percent of what students are learning today will be obsolete a decade from now, when they will be working in jobs that have yet to be created. Moore's Law isn't just changing computing power and technology or marketing; it is also affecting the education required to learn new marketing skills.

The Role of Continual Learning and Corporate Training Programs

If marketing is rapidly being transformed to look more and more like education, it made sense for me to speak to educators who are at the forefront of this transition. I spoke to three experts. The first, Ann John, is currently curriculum manager at The Flatiron School in New York City and formerly was senior manager of professional development programs at Mediabistro (where I teach online education courses on social media).

It's difficult to walk into a university setting and ask the business school to teach a class on how social data informs a company's content engagement strategy. Or how podcasting is the new networking. Or to hold a social media master class that discusses how to personally brand yourself and bring in more business through relationship economics. Ann John saw these needs and decided she wanted to be at the forefront of online education. To her, brick-and-mortar education is missing a lot of elements that online education strives to address.

Ann John thinks that because education is stuck in a four-year time frame, businesses are also stuck in a noniterative mindset. "It's hard for companies to plan out a whole year anymore," she says. "It really requires [that] a company . . . be iterative. And a lot of this comes from learning new skills." John noted that Mediabistro was established to help professionals who "didn't have time [to spend] in a conventional classroom . . . learn non conventional skills such as social media, search engine optimization, and search engine marketing." She breaks learning into two camps: informal and formal. Much of what we do on the job is the former; what we do to prepare for the future is the latter. She explained:

> [At Mediabistro,] a lot of the things we would talk about . . . with companies looking to educate their workforce had to do with a change in attitude. You can't silo disciplines into four years of learning. Learning has to be ongoing . . . throughout one's entire life cycle. I think where we're moving is [to informal] learning. If I'm at work, or I'm at school, and I have to learn to use something like Outlook, I would Google it and learn how to use [it] in real time. This is informal learning. So much happens informally that we must ask ourselves how . . . we formalize informal learning.

Ann John's points about education demonstrate the difficulty in writing a linear book on disruptive marketing—or explaining how to do it. The tactics are old by the time a person finishes reading the book. For this reason, disruptive marketing is more about personality change based on customer habits than it is about specific tactics a marketer can implement.

This is a point noted by so many others I spoke with, too. How do you change your personality from linear to dynamic? How do you leave behind the vertical thinking and doing, which is what most of conventional marketing practice consists of, to become a lateral thinker and doer? Ann continued:

> I do corporate training and the organizations that approach me are so desperate to really change their entire company's personality that they are happy to pay a lot of money for a three-hour course, [but] then that's it. This type of stop-and-go learning doesn't get to the heart of the matter. You can't say, "We'll take a three-hour course and everything will be okay." Moving forward, it has to be lifelong learning if it's going to have any true effect.

There are other, bigger issues with the value of education in improving marketing skills. For example, how do you measure the effect of skills training? Ann noted, with a heavy sigh of frustration:

> People don't want to do anything hard, which is why it's difficult to get people to adopt what amounts to a lifestyle change. Also, how do you measure the ROI of training? Turning training into small, iterative batches is a key. Many orgs don't offer any training at all, but if they did, it [would have] to be a lot like [the way] tech companies release products: not in one big release, but iterative test-and-learn phases.

Ann John steered clear of using threats, scare tactics, and "fear of missing out" messages so as to force conventional marketers to rethink their ways:

> When [your message is] "You have to keep up or you're going to be left behind," that is a bad way to frame things. It should be simpler. It should be, "You have to learn these skills to make it in the world." I think this attitude would change how people approach learning. [The purpose of] education is [to teach] how to solve a problem. It shouldn't be used [to evaluate] how well you'll do in a job. The model . . . in education is [still] . . . knowledge transfer. But that model makes no sense anymore. I learned how to think critically in college, but shouldn't I have learned that starting at age five?

Marketing's Need for Technical and Analytic Education

Ann John laid the hammer down hard on marketers who are ineffective because they lack technical prowess:

> I think in this day and age you need to know or understand a basic level of code regardless of what you are marketing. Every product, every organization . . . has a website. A website is built on code. Most people in marketing don't have that. The person making decisions in many marketing teams has no technical skills. They have a traditional background.

Geoffrey Colon
@djgeoffe

You need to learn code because code makes the world. Messages alone don't. #disruptivefm

9:33 PM—21 Feb 2016

The second person I spoke with was Allison Hemming, founder, CEO, and recruiter of the creative class. She named her firm The Hired Guns, and it's one of the top New York City firms in its field. Hemming has placed me in jobs and is always exciting to speak with; her point of view is always unique.

Allison Hemming thinks companies can't find the technical marketing talent they need, and that is a big reason some organizations are having difficulty transitioning from conventional to disruptive marketing. When listing those who have the technical marketing talent on her job board, she calls these highly sought-after candidates "mathletes." According to Hemming, "There are various things in marketing I believe are undergoing a radical shift right now. It's funny that the show *Mad Men* ended at the same time the world of marketing was undergoing the De–Don Draperization of advertising."

Geoffrey Colon
@djgeoffe

Mathletes are in high demand. They use data and creative to drive innovative marketing. #disruptivefm

9:34 PM—21 Feb 2016

In just the past five years, Hemming has seen a radical shift in who hires her firm to find talent, as well as in the jobs she lists on her weekly gig board. Hemming thinks this is because brands increasingly want people with these skill sets in-house. She explained:

> In the first five years of our existence we did a ton of agency placement work; now we are solely hired by brands and companies to place creative positions directly. Staffing has moved to the brand side.
>
> Marketing has changed; agencies were filled with creatives because they were told there was no math required in marketing. That age is gone. It's now all about accountability. If you are a marketing mathlete, you have the potential to do exceptionally well. Look at our gig board; it's all about finding people to help grow audience using analytics.
>
> If you're just starting out thinking about working in marketing, looking at positions where there [are many openings] and no [or few applicants] is a good thing. The numerative space is always going to have openings. Being predictive using analytics is something every company now wants. If you're the CMO and you're not touching data, you're not acting in the best interest of the customer. Gut-level CMOs are dinosaurs.

The Role of MBA Programs in Training Tomorrow's Marketing Talent

Glancing at one top-tiered Ivy League business school MBA schedule, I found only one class in analytics offered, while candidates were forced to take several classes on classic business theory and strategy. Much of this could be the result of a lack of qualified teachers. It might also be that education is as far behind in its understanding of what it should offer its customers—in this case, the students who shell out hundreds of thousands of dollars to earn the advanced degree.

I still find higher education amazing and worthwhile (though I may be a tad biased because my father was a political science professor), but if my father were alive and teaching, I don't know if even he would agree with an antiquated system that fails to prepare students for the lateral thinking and other skills required to live in our modern world. The third person I interviewed was Georgette

Chapman Phillips, who is dean of the College of Business and Economics at my alma mater, Lehigh University. Phillips is one of the few African American women to head a Top 50–ranked national university business school and is quite the educational futurist.

If anyone can change this way of thinking, it's Dean Phillips. On a Friday morning in Seattle I telephoned her, some three thousand some miles away on the lovely hillside campus of Lehigh University in Bethlehem, Pennsylvania. I asked her where higher education is headed, and if marketing and business students will be amply prepared for the disruptive mindset that's needed and be able to morph into the talent Hemming is seeking to place in companies.

A solid ROI seems to be at the heart of what marketing is all about now. So I wanted to know if business schools are creating a product that will provide an ROI for enrolled students. That is, if MBAs cannot prepare candidates for the new marketing organizations, is earning the degree even worth the investment? What if universities abandoned this business program for something radically different?

Phillips responded that "the [thing] that needs to be transformed quickly is the dated model of how faculty interacts with students." Talking about how technology is changing the way we learn, she added:

> I think this is one of the biggest changes . . . academia [must] face. You can be a very effective teacher by opening up your students to the same facts, day in and day out. But the four Ps (product, price, promotion, place) are not what we need to present to our students today. Our mission is to teach nuts and bolts . . . but [we must] present them in a way that they are still relevant five years from now. Our challenge in business education is to give students enough of a foundation.

I asked Phillips if universities should be offering programs in a year or two that reflect today's customer behavior. Her response reflected the urgency she feels: "We don't have to wait a year or two to offer classes on disciplines students need to learn now. If there is an area students need to learn, we roll out programs next month."

What Phillips responded sounds almost like something said by the agile engineers I speak and work with on a daily basis at Microsoft, or the many conversations I've had at startups. The difference is that instead of shipping a new product or feature to customers, Phillips is talking about shipping *education* to students as the demand necessitates. When we got into a discussion on the future of education, and how it will help students prepare for a world of disruption and disruptive marketing, her answer was what I would expect from an outfit like Mediabistro, Lynda.com, or Code Academy—not the dean of an accredited business school:

> I think education involves a lot more experiential learning. Throw students out into real scenarios and give them a safe place to swim in the marketplace. Required co-op programs. You can't learn just by reading a book anymore. Everything must be team based. Cross functionality, team-building exercises. The concept of a professor teaching students taking notes will soon be long gone. The student will do the homework in the field. This is what experiential learning is all about.

In other words, the future of education mirrors the future of marketing. "Test and learn" is the name of the game. There are no Fs or even As in these classes—just as there aren't any failures or home runs in marketing. There is only the ability to continue to adapt and learn—and then unlearn and relearn.

Learning won't be limited to four years anymore; it will be a lifelong process during which the phrase "I have twenty years of marketing experience" will be a curse, not a badge of honor unless you also have Photoshop, audio-recording, video-editing, photography, and analytical measurement skills.

EPILOGUE
FEELINGS RULE

Your intellect may be confused, but your emotions
will never lie to you.
—ROGER EBERT, movie critic

FOR MUCH OF its existence, the theory behind marketing was simple: if you have the means to create a message and the wealth to distribute it, you can control the dialogue about your company or product. When people *feel* a certain way, however, more words won't change their minds. But new feelings may.

Activist and academic Lawrence Lessig describes this effect in his book, *The Future of Ideas.* The concentration of media and distribution, he explains, would eventually falter not because of governments or regulations but because of the way disruptive marketing instills itself in our world—that is, by people inhabiting the Internet.

As I said earlier, a concentrated media world kept power and control in the hands of the few. It allowed only a few movies to be released, a certain type of music to be distributed, and only specific types of books to be published. But as Lessig notes, there was a dark side to all of this that led to a growing fragmentation of the media. More sources didn't necessarily mean better content. More cable channels didn't mean better programming. It simply allowed those cable channels to maximize their profits.

The fragmentation continues. The only blessing in this fragmentation for the field of marketing is that there is no longer an architecture that permits centralized control. Brands and organizations may continue to think they can drive the narrative, or land a message, but the new norm is about what particular kind of content or products or goals or messages or cultures or movements the marketers can inspire people to create. And most of what people will produce in the future will be very different from the mind share that companies have created in the past.

Geoffrey Colon
@djgeoffe

There is no centralization of control in the future of marketing. #disruptivefm

9:36 PM — 21 Feb 2016

There's a good reason the feelings evoked by those who have broken the grip of convention live in our hearts and not in our minds. Whether it's art or technology, or medicine or literature, the people who have dared to seek new routes have made crucial advancements in their fields that also resonate with the rest of us. Marketing is no different. And as the world continually advances, we need those who are willing to forge those new paths. Jackie Chen, a social media manager at a prominent technology company, thinks there will always be a desire for human connection, particularly as digital experiences become more sophisticated:

> I see it in the popularity of online gaming and social networks and the reach of Upworthy and TED. What we see touches us on an emotional level, which entices us to spread content because we want to have that shared experience, but we do less of that in person. Digital experiences are actually providing a way for us to feel even closer to one another. Twitch, for example, allows us to observe, yet also feel like we are part of the action.

Because human connection is so core to the human condition, there will always be a need for that human element in marketing, which will only be needed more as we spend more of our time in digital forums.

CONVENTIONAL MARKETING VS. DISRUPTIVE MARKETING

Many conventional marketers have been hesitant to make any dramatic changes to the way they orchestrate their marketing or establish their organizations. For far too long, they have been hung up on the idea that if they create content and then purchase a target audience on which to spray it, that content will somehow bring instant value to the customer. It's almost as if those marketers forgot to put themselves in the customer's shoes or to note that people aren't waiting eagerly to read, watch, or see their content (i.e., if they even notice it at all). One reason for this disconnect between content and customer is that the messages have become too complex and they present too many statistics; rather, they need to evoke emotions and feelings.

What is another big disconnect? Too much marketing is done by marketers and is not truly influenced or created by the people who use those products or identify with the company based on its ethics and the meaning that conveys. Specifically, the best marketers no longer try to get into people's heads. That is, if you want to make someone love you, make a good product.

No amount of marketing will ever make a bad product last. If you want to make a product that appeals to people, don't just rely on the engineering or development team. The disruptive marketer sits on the design team as well, and thinks of new ways to touch people's hearts.

Think about it. Why do people flock to some products like Google, but ignore other products like Bing—even if some of the former has been influenced recently by the latter's design and functionality? Is there no love of Bing? Or is it lack of awareness? Would more awareness mean anything?

To the conventional marketer, the answer is yes—more awareness is needed. To a disruptive marketer, however, the data says that more awareness isn't the answer. The answer is to spread awareness of customer love stories for the product, not more product user stats.

Perhaps David Brooks, senior vice president of digital and social strategy at Ogilvy & Mather, put it best when, during one of our many dynamic conversations about marketing, he said:

> I think things have gotten so noisy that the mind is shutting down and it is becoming even more important to reach the heart and evoke feelings. I think we remember how we feel more than what we think, but I am guessing on that. In any case, messages must evoke feelings even more than before, due to information overload; and I think even more so, messages must create a space where people can think and feel and feel inspired to create for themselves. We may be shut off from things being sent our way, but hopefully we will never shut off what we come up with on our own.

Maya Angelou, the esteemed poet and essayist, said, "I've learned that people will forget what you said, people will forget what you did, but people will never forget how you made them feel."

Geoffrey Colon
@djgeoffe

We may shut off messages directed at us but we will never shut off what we come up with on our own.
#disruptivefm

9:39 PM—21 Feb 2016

AFTERWORD

WHEN I WAS pitching this book, it dawned on me: How old does a book seem when its topic changes by the millisecond? Remaining evergreen in a world that is always on is harder and harder to do. Every day brings a new blog post, a new marketing conference presentation, a new podcast, a new video, new tweets, new Snapchats, new photos, and new infographics explaining how to best optimize the marketing in this new era. I realized the best way to do this was to provide higher-level inspirational thinking that (I hope) won't get old, because it's centered on the human experience rather than on technology or platforms; those are so "here today, gone tomorrow."

I hope that when you read this book—or reread it in 2020 or 2025—that it's still as relevant as it was in the summer of 2015 when I wrote it—although you will be reading it using virtual reality rather than your smartphone.

I didn't write this book from one location but, rather, from many locations. The best sources of inspiration are the people and things that are around us. I wrote late at night in Seattle; I also wrote in Las Vegas; San Francisco; Portland; Oregon; Brooklyn; Long Beach Island on the Jersey Shore; and at a friend's house in Maplewood, New Jersey.

I wrote it at desks, standing tables, coffeehouse cafe tables, and in a comfy chair at the house of my old friends Mike and Diedre Ayers. When I wasn't tapping away on my Windows 10–powered laptop, I was taking notes and saving them on OneNote or backing up the drafts on OneDrive. I felt I was constantly learning while I was writing. To feel and not just think, I exposed myself to as many experiences beyond the computer screen as possible. When I did foster true connection, it was with the twenty-five people I interviewed, who understood how to connect in ways we normally take for granted. Unfortunately, we tend to forget human connections in our digital distraction. We sometimes pay more attention to the computer or smartphone than to the exciting physical world and the people who inhabit it with us.

Trust me, I'm no Luddite. But trust me—reading another blog post or watching another piece of video content may not inspire you with creative ideas or flights of imagination. However, separating yourself from the world of digital devices just might. It can put into perspective what you are trying to accomplish and what your life's mission is in the creative economy—not as a marketer, but as a human being.

You may be surprised what happens when you let your heart lead the way, rather than a bunch of numbers in Hadoop without context. We have to remember that those numbers represent the actions of people, and aren't simply statistics alone. So, get outside more. Paint. Travel. Read. Observe. Love. Learn. Slam-dance. Rave. DJ. Feel. Solve math equations. Listen.

ACKNOWLEDGMENTS

I DON'T BELIEVE in individualism narratives. What I mean by this is that I don't believe an individual is solely responsible for his or her own successes or failures. I don't believe that anyone gets anything to happen of significant value by saying he did it all on his own. Unless you really believe the myth that you do everything on your own, which would mean you have zero interaction with others on this planet or you don't rely on customers that pay you a living wage, let's put an end to that mythical individualism rhetoric now.

This book is dedicated to those who saw my different thinking and doing as adding value to their companies, agencies, creative labs, or projects in the past and will see this book as adding value to their business success in the future. I learned from some of the best in the heydays of the music industry that being on top means little in a time when imaginary ideas and creativity always topple the status quo.

I want to first thank my family. My older brother Brian is my greatest mentor in terms of how I view the world. Every phone call I have with you, Brian, is meaningful; and if things remind you of our discussions, it's because those discussions have helped shape my worldview.

To my wife, Allison Dunmire. There is a reason I mention you in every public presentation. Every good idea has been your idea. I have enjoyed our journey together, exploring and learning so many new things. Life is anything but conventional with you.

To my daughters, Olive and Matilda. Your creative play is never shunned in our household in favor of mathematical tables or memorizing information. Computers can never replace creativity or human emotions. I can't wait to see what art you share with the world.

To my mother and father, who are no longer physically here. You both have been the biggest inspiration to me. My mother was a hybrid (psychology/art) who realized where the world was going and that memorizing facts and stats is useless if you can program the computer with a whole new creative way to learn and inspire. My father made me understand via economics that people, not solely companies, are what make the world tick. It's this reason I spent the majority of the book talking about people experiences as a big factor in how to approach the world.

I am especially grateful to everyone who took the time to be interviewed for the book, whether via email, a nice long phone conversation, or in person. The world is filled with really sharp and intelligent minds. We need to use these people to create things that go beyond simple vanity key performance indicators that seem to rule the world of business too much, including likes, video views, and average revenue per user stats. Let's focus instead on items like user design feedback, time spent on a video when it's replayed, and the average time users spend with product (engagement rate). These interviewees included Frank Rose, Anthony De Rosa, Steve Goldner, David Brooks, Mike Street, Julian Mitchell, Cindy Alvarez, Jennifer Moss, Matthew Woodget, Ann John, Allison Hemming, Georgette Chapman Phillips, Nicole Steinbok, Jackie Chen, Reb Carlson, Eric Drumm, Patricia MacKenzie, and Ashley McCollum.

I want to thank my friend and fellow inspirer Gemma Craven, who is one of the smartest and nicest people in the marketing industry and a true mentor. I look forward to more of our conversations soon on podcast episodes of Disruptive FM.

I thank those mentors and some of the great work I was able to do with them, including Frenzy, BOND Strategy and Influence, 360i, and Ogilvy & Mather. There are way too many individuals who have inspired this book, but a few include Jonathan Keith, Eric Cohen,

Matthew Mills, Jeffrey Boyle, Cheryl Metzger, David Schneider, Bill Crowley, Marc Schiller, Howie Kleinberg, Matt Wurst, Orli LeWinter, Sarah Hoffstetter, Michelle Killebrew, John Bell, and Joe Bua. I want to especially thank Microsoft for seeing how my different thinking could help their own transformational endeavors—especially David Pann, Stephen Sirich, John Cosley, and Rik van der Kooi. I'd also like to thank my awesome team past and present of Tina Kelleher, Simone Schuurer, Christine McClure, Frances Donegan-Ryan, Nazeem Mustaffa, Ricky Poole, and Rob Johnson. I thank Sean Ellis, Morgan Brown, Mel Carson, Joy Archer, John and Shelby Gagnon, Brian and Tracy Northcutt Toba, David Kline, Laurel Geisbush, Jay Crutcher, Christi Olson, Hannah Arussel, Sara Clayton, Esther Christoffersen, Erika Hermanns, Jimmy Lin, Connie Woo, Kerry Gates, Lucy Wang, Nickie Smith, Katy Hunter, and the hundreds of others whom I have had daily talks with in terms of the shifting marketing mindscape.

I thank my two mentors Teresa Horgan and Marja Koopmans for always lending an ear.

I thank Ellen Kadin, my publisher at AMACOM Books; and the rest of the wonderful team including Jenny Wesselmann Schwartz, Barry Richardson, Janet Pagano, and Irene Majuk. I thank my literary agent, Wendy Keller of Keller Media.

I thank Stuart Tracte for the photos for the book and my website, Jeff Gilligan for the cover art and design advice, Peter Shankman and Mel Carson for the book advice, and the endless list of people who read the book and provided advance reviews.

Finally, I want to thank some places. Yes, geographical places filled with people can influence how you think. This is why more and more people keep moving back to urban areas. Three places have given me everything: Brooklyn, New York; Maplewood, New Jersey; and Seattle, Washington. They have really helped inspire my points of view. Brooklyn in particular gave me the first business I ever operated. It made me realize the world would be mobile and social by design as early as 2002. It also has given me my life partner and a bevy of friends who are just plain amazing. Although I now call the Pacific Northwest and the great city of Seattle home, Brooklyn will always be my first true love. Maplewood, New Jersey, made me realize that the creative class can be urban/suburban and the design thinking that occurs from being a real community. Seattle just does things differently and doesn't care what others think of it.

Let's not disrupt the conversation. Follow me on Twitter, @djgeoffe; connect on LinkedIn; or visit geoffreycolon.net.

APPENDICES

TOOLS BY CATEGORY

While theory and inspiration are ways for you, the reader, to connect with me, the author, if I were to give you only theory, it wouldn't be enough. In our creative economy, we need resources to help spark ideas. This list, which is by no means exhaustive, provides some ideas for shaping your creative strategy, based on the skills described in this book, especially in chapters 6 through 9.

Keep in mind that marketers belong to the "flavor of the month" club. Agency personnel are particularly guilty of this, because they can package and sell it to their clients. Don't chase the shiny items—whether it's vertical video one day or beacon data tracking the next. Marketing, especially disruptive marketing, isn't always that disruptive once you get into the fine points—understanding people, unearthing hard-to-find insights that others simply ignore, and realizing that automation is not a threat but, rather, a way to become more important to customers. Technology is a tool; it can only help empower and execute ideas. Those ideas still need to be created by you.

DISTRIBUTION

How do you get your message heard? Reach the audience where it is. The most important application program interfaces (APIs) to learn for social network distribution include:

- Facebook Graph API
- Twitter REST APIs

PLATFORMS FOR DISTRIBUTING CONTENT

Websites with social share
   buttons: Squarespace,
   Wix, Weebly
Facebook
Twitter
LinkedIn
Instagram

Snapchat
Tumblr
Pinterest
Periscope
Streamup
Blab
Tribe

MEASURING DISTRIBUTED CONTENT

Google Analytics
Clicky
Heap
Chartbeat
Gauges
GoSquared

Calq
Indicative
Kissmetrics
Mixpanel
Trakio

HASHTAG TRACKING

Tagboard

Twubs

SEARCH ENGINE OPTIMIZATION

Moz

SEARCH ENGINE MARKETING

Bing Ads
Google Adwords
Marin

Kenshoo
Acquisio

PAID SOCIAL MEDIA

Facebook Advertising
Twitter Ads
Tumblr Advertising

Pinterest Ads
LinkedIn Ads

BLOG PUBLISHING

Medium
Wordpress

Blogger
TypePad

EMAIL MARKETING

MailChimp

Constant Contact

EMPLOYEE ADVOCACY

Sociabble   TrapIt

SOCIAL BY DESIGN

The following are ways to create that make ideas shareable:

Sight

In any essential persuasive messaging we know that we should "show, not simply tell," so in this section I've emphasized a few tools that are a big part of a disruptive marketer's arsenal.

DESIGN

Canva   Adobe Post

STOCK PHOTOGRAPHY

Shutterstock   Corbis
Getty

INFOGRAPHICS/DATA VISUALIZATION

Visual.ly   Tangle
Tableau   Polymaps
Exhibit

IMAGE TOUCHING AND ENHANCEMENT SOFTWARE

Photoshop   Paint
Apple Aperture   Pixlr
Corel PaintShop   Enlight
GIMP

PHOTO FILTERS

Ribbet   Pixlr-o-matic
Rollip

GIF CREATORS

Gifmaker   Gickr
Picasion

MEME GENERATORS

Meme Generator   Quick Meme
Meme Crunch

IMAGE-CENTRIC NETWORKS

Instagram

Tumblr

Pinterest

SlideShare

Docs.com

PRESENTATION SOFTWARE

Emaze

~~PowerPoint~~

Sway

Keynote

Camtasia

Haiku Deck

Sound

PODCASTING

Spreaker

Podbean

Soundcloud

Clammr

Jabbercast

ROYALTY-FREE MUSIC SERVICES (TO INCLUDE IN YOUR VIDEOS)

GrooveDen

Pond5

AUDIO BLOGS

Podbean

AUDIO BOOKS

Audible

Motion

NETWORKS THAT SUPPORT VIDEO

YouTube

Vimeo

SlideShare

Daily Motion

Metacafe

Blip

Keek

Vine

Instagram

PRODUCERISM

What tools can you use to create content?

SEARCH AND SOCIAL DATA (RESEARCH)

Gnip

Bing Webmaster Tools

CREATIVE INSIGHTS (RESEARCH)

Google Trends

Twitter Trending Topics

SOCIAL CRM (CUSTOMER INSIGHTS)

Sprinklr

Sprout

APPS THAT CREATE VIDEO WITH YOUR HANDSET

Videolicious

Video Star

Animoto Video Maker

Lumify

Videoshop

Facetune

iMovie

VIDEO SUBTITLING SERVICES (FOR GLOBAL AUDIENCES)

Rev

APPS OR SOFTWARE TO PRODUCE PODCASTS

Spreaker

GarageBand

Propaganda Software

POST-DIGITAL

What can you use in the physical world to reach your audience in ways
that show humanity and authenticity?

SPRAY PAINT

Krylon

Kilz (Note: only comes in
   one color—white)

Fresh Paint

Montana

Rustoleum

BOOMBOX MP3 PLAYERS

Naxa Audio

Axess Audio

Sony Audio

CASSETTE TAPES/COMPACT DISCS/VINYL-PRESSING
MANUFACTURERS

Rainbo Records

United Record Pressing

Disc Makers

MOBILE PUBLIC ADDRESS SYSTEM

AmpliVox S610A

FAX SERVICES

eFax   RingCentral

VHS TAPE/DVD DUPLICATION SERVICES

IDEA Media   Viking Video

1-800 NUMBER VOICEMAIL, VOICE BROADCASTING, OR PHONE CHAT LINES

Freedom Voice   PayPerCall.com
Access Direct

ENDNOTES

PREFACE

"When my late father, Frank, moved to Bethlehem from Pittsburgh in 1964 . . ."
John M. Lee, "1964: Year of Change for Bethlehem Steel," *New York Times*, April 12, 1964, accessed August 1, 2015, www.nytimes
.com/1964/04/12/1964-year-of-change-for-bethlehem-steel.html?_r=0

"That Music Week *article heralded the beginning of the end. . . ."*
Jack McCarthy, "Studios Sue MP3 Startup Napster," *CNN.com*, December 9, 1999, accessed July 26, 2015, www.cnn.com/1999/TECH/
computing/12/09/napster.suit.idg/

"It was too late. Like most 'sue innovation,' or what I've dubbed Californication, movements . . ."
Geoffrey Colon, "Disrupt with Californication," *LinkedIn.com*,
April 18, 2014, accessed February 27, 2016, www.linkedin.com/
pulse/20140418141623-5173732-disrupt-with-californication

"It had been known for some time—and more recently noted in Mary Meeker's 2015 Internet Trends Report. . . ."
Josh Constine, "The Mary Meeker Internet Trends 2015 Report," *Techcrunch.com*, May 27, 2015, accessed February 27, 2016, www.techcrunch
.com/2015/05/27/the-mary-meeker-internet-trends-2015-report/

INTRODUCTION

"The best marketers don't ask either/or questions. . . ."
Mark Bonchek and Cara France, "The Best Digital Strategists
Don't Think in Terms of Either/Or," *Harvard Business Review*,

June 16, 2015, accessed July 10, 2015, www.hbr.org/2015/06/
the-best-digital-strategists-dont-think-in-terms-of-eitheror

"Shaping business around real customer behavior is the challenge. . . . "
Philippa Reed, "Relinquishing Control of Your Brand: How
Digital Is Challenging Brand Building," *LinkedIn.com*, August
20, 2015, accessed August 20, 2015, www.linkedin.com/pulse/
relinquishing-control-your-brand-how-digital-challenging-reed-1

"The Socratic method is as popular as ever. . . . "
James C. Klagge and Nicholas D. Smith (ed.), *Methods of Interpreting
Plato and His Dialogues* (Oxford Studies in Ancient Philosophy, supple-
mentary volume, 1992). Oxford: Clarendon Press, 1992/

"M. Night Shyamalan did get the idea for his groundbreaking film . . . "
Stephen Adamson, "M. Night Shyamalan Got His Idea for His Best Film
'The Sixth Sense' from a Nickelodeon Show?" *Moviepilot*, July 15, 2015,
accessed August 1, 2015, moviepilot.com/posts/2015/07/30/
m-night-shyamalan-got-his-idea-for-his-best-film-the-sixth-sense-from-
a-nickelodeon-show-3427039

"Advertising agencies are also difficult to trust for innovative answers or solutions. . . . "
Murat Mutlu, "Why Talented Creatives Are Leaving Your Shitty Agency,"
Mobile Inc., September 2, 2013, accessed August 15, 2015, www.mobileinc
.co.uk/2013/09/why-talented-creatives-are-leaving-your-shitty-agency/

"In the advertising community today . . . "
David Ogilvy, "We Sell or Else," *Ogilvy One Worldwide*, October 10, 2007,
accessed August 12, 2015, www.ogilvyone.com/about/history

"Thomas Friedman wrote about just this scenario in his book The World Is Flat. . . . "
Margie Warrell, "Learn, Unlearn and Relearn: How to Stay Cur-
rent and Get Ahead," *Forbes.com*, February 3, 2014, accessed July
6, 2015, www.forbes.com/sites/margiewarrell/2014/02/03/
learn-unlearn-and-relearn/#d24365151c87

"According to Wadwha, not one industry is immune from the rapid change. . . . "
Vivek Wadwha, "2014 Is Ending, but This Wave of Technology Disrup-
tions Is Just Beginning," *Washington Post*, December 17, 2014, accessed
June 12, 2015, www.washingtonpost.com/news/
innovations/wp/2014/12/17/2014-is-ending-but-this-wave-of-
technology-disruptions-is-just-beginning/

"David Zweig, author of Invisibles: Celebrating the Unsung Heroes of the
Workplace, *declares . . . "*
David Zweig, *Invisibles: Celebrating the Unsung Heroes of the Workplace* (New
York: Portfolio, 2014), 125, 126.

"Moore's Law is used in the semiconductor industry. . . ."
Dean Takahashi, "Forty Years of Moore's Law," *Seattle Times,* April 18, 2005, accessed April 7, 2015, www.seattletimes.com/business/forty-years-of-moores-law/

CHAPTER I

"What listeners at the time did not know was that Hawthorne Court . . ."
John McDonough, "First Radio Commercial Hit Airwaves 90 Years Ago," *NPR.org,* August 29, 2012. Last modified August 30, 2012, accessed May 12, 2015, www.npr.org/2012/08/29/160265990/first-radio-commercial-hit-airwaves-90-years-ago

"Actually, the idea for radio advertising came from the telephone industry. . . ."
William Peck Banning, *Commercial Broadcasting Pioneer: The WEAF Experiment, 1922–1926* (Cambridge, MA: Harvard University Press, 1946), 3–31.

"eMarketer reports that most big brands still put a heavy emphasis on . . ."
"TV Advertising Keeps Growing as Mobile Boosts Digital Video Spend," *eMarketer.com,* April 3 2013, accessed July 19, 2015, www.emarketer.com/Article/TV-Advertising-Keeps-Growing-Mobile-Boosts-Digital-Video-Spend/1009780

"A twenty-five-year-old named Ava was interacting . . ."
Benjamin Lee, "Ex Machina stunt at SXSW Has Users Falling for a Robot on Tinder," *Guardian,* March 16, 2015, accessed May 15, 2015, www.theguardian.com/film/2015/mar/16/ex-machina-stunt-sxsw-users-falling-for-robot-tinder

CHAPTER 2

"The personality trait of a disruptive marketer is centered on what . . ."
Daniel Gilbert, *Stumbling on Happiness* (New York: Alfred A. Knopf, a division of Random House, 2006), 5.

"Google's Eric Schmidt and Jonathan Rosenberg noted . . ."
Eric Schmidt and Jonathan Rosenberg, *How Google Works* (New York, Grand Central Publishing Group, 2014), 17.

"In 2015, there were approximately 1,876 companies representing 43 different marketing . . ."
Scott Brinker, "Marketing Technology Supergraphic 2015," *chiefmartec.com,* January 2015, accessed February 28, 2016, chiefmartec.com/2015/01/marketing-technology-landscape-supergraphic-2015/

"In May 2013, I wrote a Fast Company *article, Is Content the New Currency? explaining that content . . ."*
    Geoffrey Colon, "Is Content the New Currency?" *FastCompany.com*, May 17, 2013, accessed February 28, 2016, www.fastcocreate.com/1682995/ is-content-the-new-currency

"In his influential 1937 article The Nature of the Firm, economist Ronald Coase . . ."
    Oliver E. Williamson and Sidney G. Winter, *The Nature of the Firm: Origins, Evolution and Development* (New York: Oxford University Press, 1993), 18–33.

"According to a 2014 Gartner report, . . ."
    Gartner, "70 Percent of Successful Digital Business Models to Rely on Unstable Processes That Shift with Consumers' Needs by 2017," January 22, 2015, accessed May 15, 2015, www.gartner.com/newsroom/ id/2968317

"Ray Wang, author of Disrupting Digital Business *uses scarier terminology to describe what may happen to companies. . . ."*
    Teresa Novellino, "Don't Get Cozy, Fortune 500: It's Do-or-Die time for Digital Disruption, Says This Author," *New York Business Journal*, June 4, 2015, accessed June 4, 2015, upstart.bizjournals.com/resources/ author/2015/06/04/fortune-500-must-disrupt-or-die-writes-r-ray-wang .html

CHAPTER 3

"However, in 2013, art came roaring back into many marketing campaigns. . . ."
    Alexander Jutkowitz, "Content Marketing: It's Not About Shock, but Good Storytelling," *Advertising Age*, April 9, 2013, accessed June 4, 2015, adage .com/article/cmo-strategy/content-marketing-stories-news/240776/

"In what is considered by many to be the most influential management book ever written, 1956's The Organization Man, *William H. Whyte described . . ."*
    William H. Whyte, *The Organization Man* (New York: Doubleday Anchor Books, 1957).

"Paul Mason, journalist for the Guardian, *explains it this way: . . ."*
    Paul Mason, "The End of Capitalism Has Begun," *Guardian*, July 17, 2015, accessed July 17, 2015, www.theguardian.com/books/2015/ jul/17/postcapitalism-end-of-capitalism-begun

"In the words of Lawrence Lessig, author of Remix: Making Art and Commerce Thrive in the Hybrid Economy . . ."
    Lawrence Lessig, *Remix: Making Art and Commerce Thrive in the Hybrid Economy* (New York: Penguin Books, 2008).

"Guy Debord, author and Marxist critical theorist, foreshadowed . . ."
Guy Debord, *The Society of the Spectacle* (New York: Black & Red, 2000).

"John Howkins describes the nature of this economy in his book The Creative Economy: . . .*"*
John Howkins, *The Creative Economy: How People Make Money From Ideas* (New York: Penguin Books, 2013).

"Richard Florida, author of The Rise of the Creative Class, *offers another explanation for why branding is shifting. . . ."*
Richard Florida, *The Rise of the Creative Class . . . and How It's Transforming Work, Leisure, Community & Everyday Life* (New York: Basic Books, 2003), 9.

"We're in the emerging era of what author Joshua Klein has labeled 'reputation economics.' . . ."
Joshua Klein, *Reputation Economics: Why Who You Know Is Worth More Than What You Have* (New York: Palgrave Macmillan, 2013).

"In his 2006 book, An Army of Davids: How Markets and Technology Empower Ordinary People to Beat Big Media, Big Government and Other Goliaths, *Glenn Reynolds notes . . ."*
Glenn Reynolds, *An Army of Davids: How Markets and Technology Empower Ordinary People to Beat Big Media, Big Government and Other Goliaths* (New York: Thomas Nelson, 2007).

"In fact Google's Eric Schmidt said in 2010, 'Every two days we create as much information as we did from the dawn of civilization up until 2003. That's something like five exabytes of data.' . . ."
MG Siegler, "Eric Schmidt: Every 2 Days We Create as Much Information as We Did up to 2003," *Techcrunch*, August 4, 2010, accessed August 15, 2015, techcrunch.com/2010/08/04/schmidt-data/

"Figures 3-1, 3-1a, 3-1b . . ."
"Conventional Organization Model vs. Social Network Model." Illustrations provided by Geoffrey Colon.

CHAPTER 4

"Earlier that year, the New York Times *released research on the psychology of sharing.' . . ."*
Reb Carlson, "The Psychology of Sharing," *Contently*, February 24, 2012, accessed July 1, 2015, contently.com/strategist/2012/02/24/psychology-of-sharing/

"Creativity is multidimensional and comes in many mutually reinforcing forms. . . ."
Richard Florida, *The Rise of the Creative Class . . . and How It's Transforming Work, Leisure, Community & Everyday Life* (New York: Basic Books, 2003), 5.

"In late August 2011, Chipotle released a film with Willie Nelson covering . . ."
John Bell, "Chipotle: Building Content Marketing on a Story
Platform," *The Digital Influence Mapping Project*, April 7, 2014,
accessed August 1, 2015, johnbell.typepad.com/weblog/2014/04/
chipotle-building-content-marketing-on-a-story-platform.html

"Laura Stack, author of Execution Is the Strategy, *explains that when MBAs
want only to strategize, both the organization and the individual fail. . . ."*
Laura Stack, *Execution Is the Strategy: How Leaders Achieve Maximum
Results in Minimum Time* (Oakland, CA: Berrett-Koehler, 2014).

"As of July 30, 2015, NBC/Universal was heavily invested in both BuzzFeed and Vox . . ."
Kara Swisher and Peter Kafka, "NBCUniversal Poised to Make Big Investments in BuzzFeed and Vox Media," *Re/code*, July 30, 2015, accessed
August 2, 2015, recode.net/2015/07/30/nbcuniversal-poised-to-make-
big-investments-in-buzzfeed-and-vox-media/

"Author and entrepreneur Frans Johansson has dubbed this 'The Medici Effect': . . ."
Frans Johansson, *The Medici Effect* (Cambridge, MA: Harvard Business
Review Press, 2004)

"Steve Jobs famously said, . . ."
George Beahm, *I, Steve: Steve Jobs in His Own Words* (Evanston, IL: Agate
B2 Publishing, 2011).

"In the book Free: The Future of a Radical Price, *Chris Anderson Counts the
Ways . . ."*
Chris Anderson, *Free: The Future of a Radical Price* (New York: Hyperion,
2009).

"Bruce Nussbaum, author of Creative Intelligence, *thinks so. . . ."*
Bruce Nussbaum, *Creative Intelligence: Harnessing the Power to Create, Connect, and Inspire* (New York: Harper Business, 2013).

CHAPTER 5

"We often read about the shared vision meme. . . ."
Stowe Boyd, "The Future of Engagement." *Stoweboyd.com*, June 17,
2015, accessed June 30, 2015, stoweboyd.com/post/121748537472/
the-future-of-engagement

*"What if we looked at the top five valued companies by market capitalization in
2015 again? Here's the list: . . ."*
Anne-Britt Dullforce, "FT 500 2015 Introduction and Methodology,"
Financial Times, June 19, 2015, accessed February 28, 2016, www.ft
.com/intl/cms/s/2/1fda5794-169f-11e5-b07f-00144feabdc0
.html#axzz41WLTZbPp

Financial Times FT 500 2006: Quarter One, March 31, 2006, accessed February 28, 2016, im.ft-static.com/content/images/b970931e-c2f8-11da-a381-0000779e2340.pdf

Financial Times FT 500 2006: Quarter Two, June 30, 2006, accessed February 28, 2016, im.ft-static.com/content/images/8bd31770-0a7d-11 db-b595-0000779e2340.pdf

Financial Times FT 500 2006: Quarter Three, September 30, 2006, accessed February 28, 2016, im.ft-static.com/content/images/d6af3604-51f2-11db-bce6-0000779e2340.pdf

Financial Times FT 500 2006: Quarter Four, December 31, 2006, accessed February 28, 2016, im.ft-static.com/content/images/ff835864-a646-11db-937f-0000779e2340.pdf

"In 2009, Wired *magazine featured an article entitled 'Accept Defeat: The Neuroscience of Screwing Up' that addressed . . . "*
    Jonah Lehrer, "Accept Defeat: The Neuroscience of Screwing Up," *Wired.com*, December 21, 2009, accessed August 15, 2015, www.wired .com/2009/12/fail_accept_defeat/

"That is what Dustin Wilson Sandlin—engineer and producer of YouTube channel . . . "
    Fiona Bessey-Bushnell, "The Backwards Brain Bicycle," *Scoutie Girl*, September 7, 2015, accessed September 10, 2015, www.scoutiegirl.com/the-backwards-brain-bicycle/

"Tim Brown, author of Change by Design, *describes . . . "*
    Tim Brown, *Change by Design: How Design Thinking Transforms Organizations and Inspires Innovation* (New York: Harper Business, 2009), 3–10.

"Entrepreneur and philanthropist Naveen Jain, founder of the World Innovation Institute, . . . "
    Naveen Jain, "Rethinking the Concept of 'Outliers': Why Non-Experts Are Better at Disruptive Innovation," *Forbes.com*, July 12, 2012, accessed August 1, 2015, www.forbes.com/sites/singularity/2012/07/12/rethinking-the-concept-of-outliers-why-non-experts-are-better-at-disruptive-innovation/#4ccccdf52580

CHAPTER 6

"Alec Foege, author of The Tinkerers: The Amateurs, DIYers, and Inventors Who Make America Great *best explained tinkering, . . . "*
    Alec Foege, "The Tinkerers: How Corporations Kill Creativity," *Salon .com*, December 30, 2012, accessed August 12, 2015, www.salon .com/2012/12/30/the_tinkerers_how_corporations_kill_creativity/

"Tumblr was sold to Yahoo! for $1.1 billion. . . ."
Shane Dixon Kavanaugh, "David Karp Sells Tumblr to Yahoo! for $1.1 billion," *New York Daily News*, May 19, 2013, accessed May 24, 2015, www.nydailynews.com/news/national/yahoo-acquire-tumblr-1-1-billion-article-1.1348552

"In his discussion at Ogilvy & Mather, Karp explained . . ."
Geoffrey Colon, "Tumblr CEO David Karp Speaks to Social@Ogilvy," *YouTube.com*, September 28, 2012, accessed July 6, 2015, www.youtube.com/watch?v=bXss70BpaLY

"Susan Engel, professor of psychology at Williams College, wrote about curiosity in children. . . ."
Susan Engel, "Children's Need to Know: Curiosity in Schools," *Harvard Educational Review* 81 (2011): 625–645, accessed June 11, 2015, www.academia.edu/1268822/Children_s_Need_to_Know_Curiosity_in_Schools

"In a CMO.com study, Kimberly A. Whitlere professor at University of Virginia, dissected . . ."
Kimberly A. Whitler, "2015 CMO Impact Study: Executive Summary," *CMO.com*, May 2015, accessed June 10, 2015, www.cmo.com/content/dam/CMO_Other/articles/2015CMOImpactStudy/2015CMOImpactStudy_ExecutiveSummary.pdf

"David Packard, cofounder of Hewlett Packard, said . . ."
Ira Kalb, "You Have to Be a Little Crazy To Be a Marketing Consultant," *Huffington Post*, May 19, 2015, accessed May 31, 2015, www.huffingtonpost.com/ira-kalb/you-have-to-be-a-little-c_b_7337630.html

"I first read about this philosophy in the 2010 book Rework, *by Jason Fried and David Heinemeier Hansson. . . ."*
Jason Fried and David Heinemeier Hansson, Rework (New York: Crown Business, 2009), 193–194.

"Created by John D. Mayer, of the University of New Hampshire, and Peter Salovey, of Yale, has come to be defined as . . ."
John D. Mayer, Peter Salovey, David R. Caruso, "Emotional Intelligence: Theory, Findings, and Implications," *Psychological Inquiry*, 15 (2004) 197–215.

CHAPTER 7

"Ian penned a piece on Medium *entitled 'WTF is Social Media Anyway?' that gets to the heart. . ."*
Ian Schafer, "WTF is Social Media Anyway?" *Medium.com*, August 10, 2015, accessed August 10, 2015, ianschafer.com/wtf-is-social-media-anyway-4862507b63bb

"Who wouldn't wouldn't want to be in a company now valued at $850 million?. . . ."
  Peter Kafka, "NBCUniversal Buys Big Chunks of Vox
  Media and BuzzFeed," *Re/code*, August 12, 2015, accessed August 12, 2015, recode.net/2015/08/12/
  nbcuniversal-buys-big-chunks-of-vox-media-and-buzzfeed/

"Figure 7-1: BuzzFeed Marketing Feedback Loop. . . ."
  Image redrawn and designed by author with permission by Ashley
  McCollum of BuzzFeed, *Buzzfeed.com*, 2015.

"Chris Anderson touched on this in his 2006 book, The Long Tail: *. . ."*
  Chris Anderson, *The Long Tail: Why the Future of Business Is Selling Less of
  More* (New York: Hyperion, 2005), 83–84.

"Figure 7-2: The Architecture of Participation. . . ."
  Image courtesy of Chris Anderson and The Long Tail Blog. Chris
  Anderson, "The New Architecture of Production," *longtail.typepad.com*,
  August 2, 2005, accessed June 7, 2015, longtail.typepad.com/the_long_
  tail/2005/08/the_new_archite.html

*"In 2014, Edison Research found that 39 million Americans had listened to a pod-
cast in the previous month. . . ."*
  Nancy Vogt, "Podcasting Fact Sheet," *Pew Research Center*, April 29,
  2015, accessed May 1, 2015, www.journalism.org/2015/04/29/
  podcasting-fact-sheet/

CHAPTER 8

*"If Mitchell's predictions are correct, could our lives look like the one depicted in one of
the most controversial documentaries ever created,* We Live in Public. *. . ."*
  We Live in Public. "Watch the We Live in Public Movie Trailers,"
  accessed February 27, 2016, weliveinpublic.blog.indiepixfilms.com/

"In 1998, MIT Media Lab cyber pundit Nicholas Negroponte pointed out in Wired
magazine, . . ."
  Nicholas Negroponte, "Beyond Digital," *Wired.com*, December 1, 1998,
  accessed July 1, 2015, www.wired.com/1998/12/negroponte-55/

CHAPTER 9

"In one of the film's most intense scenes . . ."
  Roger Ebert, "Glengarry Glen Ross," October 2, 1992, accessed June 12,
  2015, www.rogerebert.com/reviews/glengarry-glen-ross-1992

"Just don't tell Ken Wheaton, managing editor of Advertising Age. *Wheaton wrote a 2015 op-ed. . . ."*

Ken Wheaton, "Forget Disruption, Just Get Better at Interruption," *Advertising Age,* July 13, 2015, accessed July 13, 2015, adage.com/article/ ken-wheaton/focusing-disruption-interruption/299447/

"Susan Cain noted this powerful philosophy in her must read book, Quiet: The Power of Introverts in a World That Can't Stop Talking.*"*

Susan Cain, Quiet: *The Power of Introverts in a World That Can't Stop Talking* (New York: Broadway Books, 2012), 21, 51.

"Figure 9-1 Data Never Sleeps 2.0, 2011-2013"

Image courtesy of Domo.com, accessed March 17, 2016, www.domo. com/learn/data-never-sleeps-2

CHAPTER 10

"Capgemini, a French consulting technology corporation, defines AAS . . ."

Capgemini.com, "Insights as a Service," accessed June 13, 2015, www .capgemini.com/insights-data/insights/insights-as-a-service

CHAPTER 11

"Buycott is a mobile app created by Ivan Pardo, a Los Angeles–based developer. . . ."

Clare O'Connor, "New App Lets You Boycott Koch Brothers Monsanto and More by Scanning Your Shopping Cart," *Forbes.com,* May 14, 2013, accessed July 23, 2015, www.forbes.com/sites/ clareoconnor/2013/05/14/new-app-lets-you-boycott-koch- brothers-monsanto-and-more-by-scanning-your-shopping-cart/

"My colleague Lin Huang at Bing Ads recently studied. . ."

Lin Huang "How Social Signals Affect Brand Reputation." Paper presented at Search Marketing Exposition Advanced, Seattle, Washington, June 2–3, 2015, www.slideshare.net/SearchMarketingExpo/ how-social-signals-affect-brand-reputation-by-lin-huang

"To test this theory I sometimes ask my Millennial friends . . ."

"Steve Ballmer quotes," *Searchquotes.com,* accessed August 12, 2015, www. searchquotes.com/quotation/We've_grown_from_18%25_of_the_ profits_of_the_top_25_companies_in_our_industry_to_23%25_of_the_ profits_of/45306/

" . . . seven out of ten Millennials regard themselves as social activists, according to a 2011 study by TBWA/Worldwide. . . ."

Mitch Nauffts, "[Infographic] The Future of Social Activism," *Philanthropy News Digest,* September 21, 2013, accessed July 21, 2015, pndblog.typepad .com/pndblog/2013/09/infographic-the-future-of-social-activism.html

CHAPTER 12

"Phillips is one of the few African American women to head a Top 50–ranked national university business school. . . ."
Gwen Moran, "The Dean Reinventing the MBA Program and Challenging Diversity Assumptions," *FastCompany.com,* March 9, 2015, accessed April 18, 2015, www.fastcompany.com/3043248/strong-female-lead/lehigh-universitys-new-dean-on-challenging-diversity-assumptions

EPILOGUE

"Activist and academic Lawrence Lessig describes this effect in his book, The Future of Ideas. *The concentration of media and distribution . . ."*
Lawrence Lessig, *The Future of Ideas: The Fate of the Commons in a Connected World* (New York: Vintage, 2002), 119.

ADDITIONAL READING

The following are ten books you should also read to become a disruptive marketer:

1. *I Live in the Future and Here's How It Works: Why Your World, Work, and Brain Are Being Creatively Disrupted,* Nick Bilton (New York, Crown Business, an imprint of the Crown Publishing Group, a division of Random House, Inc., 2010).
2. *How Google Works,* Eric Schmidt and Jonathan Rosenberg (New York, Grand Central Publishing, a division of Hachette Book Group, Inc., 2014).
3. *The Rise of the Creative Class . . . and How It's Transforming Work, Leisure, Community, and Everyday Life,* Richard Florida (New York, Basic Books, 2002).
4. *Blink: The Power of Thinking Without Thinking,* Malcolm Gladwell (New York, Little, Brown and Company, 2005).
5. *The Lean Startup: How Today's Entrepreneurs Use Continuous Innovation to Create Radically Successful Businesses,* Eric Ries (New York, Crown Business, 2011).
6. *The Long Tail: Why the Future of Business Is Selling Less of More,* Chris Anderson (New York, Hyperion, 2006).
7. *The Wisdom of Crowds,* James Surowiecki (New York, Anchor Books, 2004).

8. *A Whole New Mind: Why Right-Brainers Will Rule the Future,* Daniel H. Pink (New York, Riverhead Books, 2005, 2006).

9. *The Design of Business: Why Design Thinking Is the Next Competitive Advantage,* Roger Martin (Cambridge, MA, Harvard Business Press, 2009).

10. *Originals: How Non-conformists Move the World,* Adam Grant (New York, Viking, 2016).

INTERVIEWEES

STEVE GOLDNER — SocialSteve.wordpress.com

FRANK ROSE — author, *The Art of Immersion: How the Digital Generation Is Remaking Hollywood, Madison Avenue, and the Way We Tell Stories*

ANTHONY DE ROSA — former editor for Reuters and Circa; digital production manager, *The Daily Show* with Trevor Noah

DAVID BROOKS — senior vice president, Ogilvy & Mather

TRICIA MacKENZIE — director of marketing & communications, Boston College Center for Corporate Citizenship

NICOLE STEINBOK — senior program manager, Surface at Microsoft

DAVID KARP — founder of Tumblr

IAN SCHAFER — CEO and founder of Deep Focus

MICHAEL STREET — digital/social strategist, Burrell Communications, and podcaster of SmartBrownVoices

JULIAN MITCHELL — senior branded writer, BuzzFeed

ALLISON HEMMING — CEO, The Hired Guns

JACKIE CHEN — social media manager

REB CARLSON — social media manager, Master Dynamic; past work at Sprinklr

ERIC DRUMM — digital strategist, GLOW Digital Agency

MATTHEW WOODGET — storyteller, Microsoft

GEORGETTE CHAPMAN PHILLIPS — dean, College of Business and Economics, Lehigh University

TANNER CHRISTENSEN — product designer, Facebook

ASHLEY MCCOLLUM — vice president, Business Development and Communications, BuzzFeed

ANN JOHN — curriculum manager, The Flatiron School

JENNIFER MOSS — cofounder, Plasticity

CINDY ALVAREZ — director, Yammer

DONA SARKAR — principal program manager, Microsoft Hololens

SCOTT LUM — content marketing and social media strategist

MATT WALLAERT — behavioral scientist, Microsoft Ventures

ABOUT THE AUTHOR

GEOFFREY COLON is communications designer and social data expert at Microsoft in Bellevue, Washington. The majority of his work concentrates on growth marketing for Microsoft search advertising products, using social data and digital tools. Geoffrey leads a scrum team of disruptive marketers who create, execute, and measure 50/50 "creative meets analytical" strategies to help drive education, adoption, connection, and cultural immersion for the Bing Ads product with advertisers. He is also a subject-matter expert on personal branding, the gig economy, socializing the enterprise, the future of work, content marketing, and podcasting.

Prior to joining Microsoft in 2013, Geoffrey was vice president of digital strategy at Ogilvy & Mather, in New York City. In that role, Geoffrey created and executed tactical social strategies for IBM. He authored several of the top thought-leadership pieces for the agency, including one on content as the new currency for Fast Company.

Geoffrey has spent twenty years in various marketing capacities working for and with several of the most influential brands, including IBM, Red Bull, Spotify, Netflix, the *Economist*, and the Food Network. He spent a few years in the startup world and several years in the music industry as DJ Geoffe, during which time he released over a dozen commercially available mix compilations. He has also worked with several high-profile musical artists, including Britney Spears, Christina Aguilera, The White Stripes, and Moby.

Geoffrey is a 1994 graduate of Lehigh University with a bachelor of arts degree in journalism and mass communications. He is host of the weekly marketing podcast for eccentric minds *Disruptive FM* and blogs regularly on DisruptiveMarketer.net. He also contributes original articles regularly to LinkedIn, Medium, and the Microsoft Search Advertising blog. He has been quoted in various publications and media outlets, including *Marketplace* on NPR, the *Wall Street Journal, Billboard Magazine,* the *Los Angeles Times, Advertising Age,* and *Digiday,* and is an avid speaker on the global marketing conference circuit. This is his first book.

INDEX